"I am always in awe of writers brave enough to reach back into their childhoods and revisit the unalterable pain of becoming a human in the world. *Funeral for Flaca* does so fearlessly and generously: Emilly Prado's writing is a panorama of the often harsh landscape that made her a storyteller, and of the bonds—of family, culture, self-knowledge, and justice—that propel her forward."
—Andi Zeisler, author of *We Were Feminists Once*, co-founder of *Bitch Media*

"*Funeral for Flaca* isn't just stories—it's also a mixtape, delivering beautifully-rendered stories to a soundtrack. The book shares experiences that anyone who's been a kid could recognize."
—"State of Wonder" *Oregon Public Broadcasting*

"I felt invited to join Emilly Prado on her journey. Reading *Funeral for Flaca* felt like music feels when you are intoxicated; I found myself picking this book up even when I thought I was done reading for the day. I felt engulfed in her world. I understood her stories in a very intimate way that only others who share a similar journey to your own can reflect. It is a beautiful book, told phenomenally."
—Prisca Dorcas Mojica Rodríguez, author of *For Brown Girls with Sharp Edges and Tender Hearts: A Love Letter to WOC*

"Tender and tough, these intimate essays trace Prado's life and key experiences that have shaped her. So many essays explore embodiment in a heartfelt and nuanced way, both a sense of discomfort and finding peace despite this. There is rarely a neat and simple resolution." —Alicia Kroell, Catapult Books

"I will never be the same now that I've read it. It's doing exactly what books were built to do—to challenge, explain, and bring new layers of empathy to the human experience." —Sara Guest, author of *White Cities*

FUNERAL FOR FLACA

essays

EMILLY G. PRADO

Future Tense Books

Portland, Oregon

ISBN: 978-1-892061-87-4

Edited by Kevin Sampsell and Emma Alden. Proofread by Sara Guest. Layout by Michael Kazepis. Cover design by Francisco Morales.

First edition. Printed in the United States of America.

Published by Future Tense Books.
www.futuretensebooks.com
Portland, Oregon

Para las Marias.

TRACKS

00. intro

I DIDN'T GROW up believing I could be a writer. In my fifth-grade yearbook, I am quoted saying I'd like to become a "soccer player/singer/entertainer" when I grew up—the *entertainer* deliberately vague as to hold space for acting and dancing. I had secretly dreamt of being an author once or twice when I was little—of holding a book in my hands with a spine that said "By Emilly Prado"—but I never actually thought it would be something I could accomplish within my lifetime. Kid me had a hard time believing I was smart enough or had a story worth telling. Young adult me had a hard time believing the same, on top of the added doubts that writing was financially feasible. And yet here I am, almost 30, having written, rewritten, and compiled years of vulnerable, embarrassing, emotional, sometimes funny personal essays into one place.

Funeral for Flaca is a collection of essays about growing up. It's about learning to navigate change, identity, and building self-worth. It's about traumas, and the ways our bodies, communities, and brains respond. My pathway to writing has been winding, but ever-present. I participated in a prose and bookmaking certificate program that met weekly at the Independent Publishing Resource Center (IPRC) with Margaret Malone from 2018-19, and it was the longest concentrated time I've yet spent developing my craft and focused only on creative writing. I was named the Debby Rankin scholar for the year, and this was vital in making studying writing financially possible. The culmination of my time was a handmade, self-published marigold collection made with cardstock, Photoshop, risograph, InDesign, a guillotine paper slicer, shimmery gold accent paper, and with plenty of folks' help along the way whether to read, edit, fact check, or help hot glue the spines (and subsequently hand model on my Instagram stories). My community, and family, has consistently showed up to support my continued pursuit of writing whether through buying my zines and letterpress prints, donating to fundraisers in support of a writing workshop, showing up to readings, spreading the word of classes I'm teaching or of my newsletter, or just being there to talk through next steps.

A Facebook thread connected me with Kevin Sampsell who has spent many years supporting new authors like me as the small press curator and bookseller at Powell's Books, and as the publisher at Future Tense Books. Kevin agreed to sell my slightly wonky-but-pretty memoir-in-essays fresh out of the IPRC and was one of many people who helped me believe this collection was worth sharing. As you can see now, as you hold this book, Kevin also invested in helping my debut collection reach a wider audience in this revised and gleefully expanded version of *Funeral for Flaca* with Future Tense Books!

My very first introduction to writing, outside of school, was as a tool where I learned how to vent and process. My oldest sister, Erika, gifted me a hardcover, pastel blue-and-cream diary with Japanese stab binding when I'd just entered middle school. The cover had pressed flowers and its interior was filled with thick, textured pages. It was both delicate and strong, and it felt safe. I learned to jot down what happened in my day and found a space to experiment with being reckless or careful with my words. I'd write about the rage that boiled up from my stomach into my throat—the rage that choked me up to the point of silence and tears for many years until I went through anger management (twice) and learned how to talk through my emotions. I remember feeling like writing was the only way I could say exactly what I wanted to say, how I wanted to say it. I could fully use my voice without all the baggage that seemed to come with attempting to use my speaking voice. In particularly stressful or emotional times, I'd write letters to people and hand them over instead of trying (and failing) to speak. I eventually learned how to write *and* speak what I was feeling, in great part thanks to my diary.

I was also inspired to write by Tupac Amaru Shakur. His music saved me, as you'll read, and was foundational to my radicalization. *The Rose that Grew from Concrete* showed me I could write about my life through poetry, like Pac. I could use slang and shorthand too—I didn't have to speak like Shakespeare to be a writer. I also give thanks to my beloved Mami for fostering my love in music of many genres, and for helping me refine my selection skills. She passed down her own excellent, varied musical sensibilities to me, and explained to me early on that I needed to create *flow* in my mix CDs. "Dixie Chicks shouldn't come immediately after 'Slow Motion' by Juvenile, or even before Linkin Park," she once said.

I developed a penchant for compiling my favorite age-inappropriate slow jams and would burn extra copies for my friends. I'd swap mixes with any and every cousin or classmate. When CDs became passé, I made iTunes playlists to woo high school boyfriends. We'd each take an iPod ear bud and listen to the mixes during lunch. When we'd break up, I'd blast tear-jerker R&B hits like Mariah Carey's "We Belong Together" or Amanda

Perez's "Angel" from my bedroom boombox and I'd let the tears flow with abandon. After my first post-college relationship fizzled, I made an online series of public breakup playlists on Tapely for every mood (sadness by genre, different songs to be pissed to, hell-yes-I'm-single vibes, and more).

Music and writing have always been there for me when I needed to feel seen, and not so alone. They've both gifted me a perpetual source of joy, hope, and release. I feel lucky to share these mediums with others through my writing and DJing, and I've tried to channel that energy into this book. *Funeral for Flaca* is a personal essay collection, but it's also part mixtape. I've picked beloved songs as the titles of each chapter. You can listen to most of the songs online at tinyurl.com/flaca-playlist. I've added title songs first, followed by any other songs mentioned in the essays, and a few bonuses.

There's a practice of asking authors who their books have been written for—who the audience they had in mind when they were clacking away on their keyboards. I think I have given many answers to this question in the past: for all marginalized people, for my Abuelita Maria, for *everyone*, but the person I keep coming back to is 13-year-old Emilly. This was the first age I knew the emptiness of what having no hope at all feels like. This was thankfully the age I was also pulled to the foundations I would continue to center in my life—writing, music, questioning and seeking justice, looking for ways to feel better about myself and my role in this world. There are parts of me that are still afraid to share the words in this book more widely—afraid they will be judged, or worse, cause any hurt, but I know these are the memories I needed to excavate and, in some ways, lay to rest.

This is still the beginning of my journey as a storyteller, and like the diary excerpts in this book I find peace knowing what I've poured into these pages and this collection is a time capsule in itself. These are the reflections tethered to my now—reflections that have changed immensely, even since the first iteration of this book two years ago.

I dearly wish I had more books that felt accessible and relevant for me when I was thirteen. Books that I didn't need to bust out the dictionary for, that I didn't need to guess too hard to deduce the meaning. It's not that I don't love books like that—I do—and I promise there are messages and themes to be read between the lines, but I wanted *Funeral for Flaca* to be told in a way that 13-year-old me might read as heavy and perhaps not totally understand, but could read knowing it was real. There is so much beauty in sharing the sweet, tender moments of life that make it feel like a dream. There is also so much beauty in sharing realness.

Funeral for Flaca progresses as chronologically as possible from about 1995 to 2021. Some sentences are direct quotes from old diary entries, many more than a decade old. All the essays are about trying to make sense of my emotions, the world, and my place in it. The words trace my metamorphosis. I hope this collection offers you nectar.

01. say you'll be there

I DON'T REMEMBER if I picked Krista Landers to be my best friend or if she picked me. But in kindergarten, Krista Landers and I made a promise to be best friends forever. For picture day, Krista's mom dressed her in big bows and burgundy plaid with her blonde hair cut in a fresh bob. My Mami dressed me in a single big bow, black Dalmatian dress, and my long black hair in a wavy half-up pony, tied back with a string of Flea Market bolitas.

When my family arrived in Belmont, we were starting new. My Mami and Papi, adult GED earners, tell me, now, they wanted their kids to grow up in a place where college was the norm. Papi doesn't actually tell me this—only my mom does. But I like to imagine there was a point in their relationship when they agreed and made decisions about their life together like this. So, Redwood City was out, and Belmont was supposed to be home now.

Krista and I both had little brothers. Our brothers would also become fast friends. When Krista and I met, our parents were all still together, too. I don't remember what we bonded over first, but our BFF bond would last us almost all the way through high school.

Cuando empecé kinder, I mostly only spoke español. I'd ask my Mami, "Cuál estoy hablando ahora?" "What about now?" and I suppose I did this until my tongue learned which way to dance for different people. Kindergarten was the first time I was in school for a whole year—my two stints in preschool were cut short. My Mami said I became fluent in English in three months. No recuerdo when my thoughts, mi lengua, followed suit. I don't remember when I stopped dreaming in Spanish.

* * *

Mrs. Maier picked popsicle sticks out of a jar at the end of show-and-tell for the next show-and-tell every Friday. Our whole class huddled in a circle around the giant flat pile rug, eyes wide and our stomachs full of mariposas, as we waited for who would be called next. We each had a popsicle stick in there that was *ours*. One popsicle stick—permanently marked—with our names in thick black Sharpie. Me and Krista always sat next to each other atop the cobalt monstrosity. Sometimes we'd hold hands. Mrs. Maier would shake up this jar of popsicle sticks, each piece of wood crashing into the others, fighting for luck.

"Krista," Mrs. Maier said one fateful Friday with her small lips puckered up, eyebrows raised. She leaned into the mystery of the charade and seemed to look every pupil in the eye each time she waved that first popsicle stick in the air.

"Aaand. . ."

Mrs. Maier always let it linger.

Por favor Dios. Pick me.

"—Emilly," she finally said.

Yesss!

* * *

In kindergarten, the rest of elementary school, and part-way through sixth grade, I was known as Emily, one L. Neither my Mami nor my Papi remembered the momentous typo they made in the wee madrugada of July, but their choices point to liking of Ls. I think we agree about the loopty elegance of Ls. Emilly Giselle Prado. Twice as many Ls any other girl by the same name might have, twice as much frill, twice as much.

Emilly. Our American Dream version of *Emiliana,* the true feminine equivalent of my namesake, *Emiliano.* My tragically murdered-in-his-20's uncle. A deal-gone-wrong gunshot to the head on a park bench, one sunny afternoon. A patron saint to the Prado's. An easy person to point to as one part of my Papi's downfall with my mother.

Like my double Ls, I remember Papi having twice as many phones as one might expect when I was growing up. He said he was an entrepreneur. *I thought entrepreneur meant he had a lot of jobs.* He said he had cows in Mexico. *I had seen them.* He said he owned grocery stores with Tia Isela and Chuck. *I had been to them.* In Aguililla, where the cattle roamed our rancho and were herded by Papa Nano—big Emiliano—I learned to say I was my father's daughter whenever another kid was teasing me. I thought we might be famous, or at least special in some way? Our name was whispered and repeated in a way that made us sound like lore.

In Belmont, California, 94002, no one seemed to know us besides our family. Eventually other kids at school knew us, but no one looked like us there. The brown kids—two of which were me and my sister Erika—could be counted on one hand. I think the Black student(s) could be counted with two or fewer fingers.

I have a hard time remembering everything I thought, everything that was said, which sides of which stories were real, but I know Mami picked me up from school most days and some days, when my Papi was in town, he'd be the one to drive me. I'd hold his hand the whole way to the car. We'd ride in his maroon Jeep and—pre-weight limits and safety laws—my kindergarten body would buckle up in shotgun. We'd listen to Wild 94.9 or Amor 100.3.

One time, Ms. Crane, the always-annoyed, cock-eyed teacher whose class was next door to Mrs. Maier's tried to stop me and my Papi from going home. She thought he was a *stranger*. I thought her spikey white hair made her look like a witch struck by lightning, or maybe she got shocked from sticking a fork in an outlet like my right-hand-turned-left-handed cousin.
Getting picked up by Papi was something exceptional, something sweet. In addition to his presence, I would often get another surprise: a McDonald's happy meal with plenty of extra fancy ketchup packets, a new Barbie, or maybe a new set of rainbow bolitas. I felt so loved when he picked me up. I felt so loved when I got to ride in the car with my Papi.

* * *

Me and Krista whispered ideas for show-and-tell on the cobalt carpet and in the line for the bathroom and on the kindergarten-only playground outside. We wanted to *wow* our classmates. We wanted to win show-and-tell.

If we had been picked for 'B,' we would have brought each other (Best Friends) even though Connor and Taylor did that first. If we had gotten 'C,' I would have brought in my Spice Girls CD and Krista would've brought in her Backstreet Boys one. But we were dealt the letter 'D.' I didn't have a dog. I really loved drawing, but I thought that would be boring because I couldn't pencil draw horses good like Courtney. I couldn't think of what might possibly top bringing another kid in our classroom as a show-and-tell item?

Then one day Krista said she had a good idea. She tried to get me to guess.

"It's someone who doesn't even have Mrs. Maier or go to Garibaldi Elementary," she said.

I was stumped.

"A *dad*," Krista explained.

My eyes got big. That *was* a good idea. I didn't tell her I called my dad *papi*—but I still thought we could win.

When I asked my Papi if he could pretty please come into class next week for show-and-tell, I was bursting, could barely get the sentences out; I was so giddy!

"Claro que si, mi Flaca," he said, and I thought I'd explode into bits right in that Jeep.

* * *

The week zipped by and, somehow, it was Friday again. I selected my favorite Old Navy bell bottom pants with cute cheetah heart patches to wear. I made sure to ask Mami to wash them the night before for the special occasion, because one time, I tried shoving them into a drawer to skip the weekly cycle, didn't trick her, and I had to wear less-cool pants. This was a day for cool pants.

Mami has always known how to make special days feel a little more special. One of my favorite ways Mami tells me I am loved is with her mini burritos con jamon y huevo. She makes these with flour tortillas for a breakfast on-the-go. I liked, and still like, to hold them with two hands to warm me up. I'd move the soft, sometimes crispy burrito skin right under my nose to take a whiff before attempting a huge first bite. The attempt at *huge* is crucial because I have always disliked a tortilla-only first mouthful. I also learned to be *careful* because the folded tortilla's tendency to spring out like a jack-in-the-box can hurl the huevo. My Mami and Papi had no interest in raising messy girls.

"—'Member today is show-and-tell," I said to my Papi on the winding drive to school, full from Mami's food. "Today is the Big Day."

"Si, M'ija!" he said with a smile, eyes looking at the street. I swear it felt like we always caught air up and down those hills.

One of Papi's phones rang, and he answered it.

We arrived at Garibaldi. I kissed him goodbye on the cheek while he was still talking.

At Friday morning circle, the mariposas were back in my stomach. The mariposas knew Krista's and my secret. Krista confirmed her dad, Frank, was definitely coming in soon for show-and-tell. My Papi, named Hector like both of my baby brothers, said he was coming in too, I reported back. *Two best friends with two dads for show-and- tell.* It really was the perfect plan.

One circle time before our Friday, my tummy had been bubbling up on the big blue rug. In the dead silence the bubbles escaped from my butt, and I accidentally farted—LOUD. All the kids knew it was me—the noise, the direction was so clear—and laughed. I think some of them laughed until they were crying. I would have laughed if it wasn't me, but it was me! So, I turned into Mrs. Maier' arm, pushed my face into the soft between her elbow, and cried that day. For *my* show-and-tell Friday, I pledged to keep in all my farts in.

I think we followed up the morning circle with our regular schedule of the day. It's impossible to remember the order, but I am sure the morning included telling Mrs. Maier about the weather and someone in my class unsticking and then sticking the Velcro orange sun again on the felt poster at the front of the class. We'd work on our rote memorization—adult me questions the pedagogy, but kid me ate it up. We'd sing our memorized songs back as a class, and I think all students would agree that none was more iconic than the poem, "There Once Was a Puffin." *Oh, there once was a puffin just the shape of a muffin and it lived on an island in the bright blue sea. It ate little fishes that were most delicious, and it had them for supper and it had them for tea. . .*

I am sure there were other things happening that day besides show-and-tell, but all I could see, or think about, was show-and-tell. Everything else was in the way. It was always before recess at 10:00AM. *Why did 10:00AM feel so long?* Maybe we wrote in our journals or got started on building a small village out of milk cartons. I was probably having fun, but I am sure I kept one eye on the clock, watching the numbers crawl until the 10 o'clock hour arrived.

When it was 10:00, we all knew what to do next: line up, single file, and wash our hands at one of two sinks. I saw Krista's dad's eyes peek through the window on the classroom door as I rubbed soap in my palms. He was *right* on time. Then I watched as Mrs. Maier's assistant teacher went out to talk to him, and I watched how none of the other kids noticed her move past them. The assistant teacher came back in, but Krista's dad did not. How were adults always so good at being stealth?

I whispered to Krista what I'd seen, hands cupped around her ear, protecting the secret from escaping. Her eyebrows squirmed with excitement, and we both smiled.

Mrs. Maier whispered to me, asking if my dad was still coming.

"He is coming!" I told her. "Just wait."

* * *

I figured out Santa Claus was fake when I was maybe six. The idea of a big man wiggling down into a chimney with an even wider load of gifts sounded far-fetched. The flying around the world on a sled pulled by reindeer? Something I wanted to believe could be real, even though my gut told me it wasn't possible. But just maybe it was a type of magic, like God.

I'd ask my Mami and Papi if Santa Claus was real, and they'd say yes yes—*claro que si.* I'd remind Mami that we had to leave out milk and cookies, and something about the adults not remembering to do this without me asking made me think it was all a little suspicious. Didn't they know naughty was the exact opposite of being nice?!

One night near Christmas Eve—Mexican families' midnight equivalent a Christmas morning gift opening—I devised a stake out. After Mami tucked me into bed with my sister, I tip-toed through the dark hall, hiding behind the entry to the bathroom, before I looked both ways and jumped past the dining room table. I crawled through the dining room, using the dining table first then a console table as cover, all the way near the couch, TV, and Christmas tree area. I sidled up into the dark slit between the arm of our couch and the wall and waited. Mami and Papi were fussing with stuff near the tree. Papi was stacking the gift boxes and Mami headed back to the dining room table *(close call)*. She pulled reems of shiny red and strands of green, and Scotch taped a box all over. Then Papi put it under the tree.

"HA! I caught you!" I screamed, cackling.

"I knew Santa wasn't real!"

My Mami and Papi said something about being Santa's helpers. I remember thinking it felt like a possible answer, but it didn't exactly add up. When I argued back and they gave up, I knew my eyes were right. Little Hector didn't figure out Santa Claus was fake until we told him when he was 11 years old.

* * *

At show-and-tell time, we sat in a circle on the big blue rug. Kids took turns standing up at the front of the class. The rules of show-and-tell meant kids could sit with their backpacks on—usually not allowed—but had to wait for Mrs. Maier's signal to open them up.

Dougie opened his red Power Rangers backpack and pulled out Uno cards. Someone yelled it didn't count (I was thinking the same), and Dougie said it was a "*deck*."

Everyone shut up when Dougie gave out a card for each to hold. Sometimes the show-and-tell items are boring, but the Uno deck was clever. As much as the cards were fun to pass around, I was getting antsy. I looked at the door and I looked to the windows. I didn't see my Papi's eyes yet.

More show-and-tells happened, and suddenly Mrs. Maier said it was Krista's turn. I asked her to wait—just a little bit longer, *please*. I knew it was going to be so much cooler to have our dads come in together. Mrs. Maier looked right in my eyes and said Sarah could go, but Krista would go next. This is the point when I really started to feel nervous.

I still hadn't seen my dad. I tried to get up, mid-Sarah presentation, to look around for him. Maybe he was outside?

But the assistant teacher and her daddy long legs got her to the door more quickly. "He isn't here yet," she said to me.

It was 10:25AM, and I knew show-and-tell would end at 10:30AM. I understood five minutes meant *soon.*

Mrs. Maier said Krista would go up first, but I could go at a special time later in the day. HE IS COMING, I wanted to scream. I felt the tingles dancing up and down my throat, the warmth swirling in my chest. The blush buried behind my brown cheeks. I hated it.

Krista was excited. I wanted to be excited. She hopped up to the front of the room and asked, "Are you ready for my show-and-tell?" to the whole class. She had no backpack in hand, no arm tucked behind her in fake secrecy. Everyone was hooked. I tried to be excited too.

"Okay, here it is!" she said.

She skipped to the door. The door suddenly felt so far away. The room was so quiet.

She twisted the silver knob and pushed it wide open.

Krista's dad stepped in with the biggest smile I have ever seen. He had a contagious smile and was always a flirt with other moms in a way that somehow never quite came off as creepy— only funny. I think it was what moms called *charm*. Even now, if I picture Frank's smile, I think of his crow's feet, tan bed cheek lines, chiseled chin above a bush of chest hair, and hella goofy laugh.

But in that moment, I remember my mouth did not want to make a smile. I still tried.

"This is my Dad," Krista said, smile matching Frank's dazzling whites.

I can't remember how much longer I waited before shouting out, "My Dad is coming too! He's just late." I don't think it was long enough. I don't think the kids heard me. When Mrs. Maier looked me in the eyes, I knew she had.

Kids asked Krista's dad questions. They wanted to know where he worked. How many kids he could carry? How many years had he been on earth? I wanted to ask my dad just one question—*Where was he?* This was the point when I wanted to cry.

* * *

Mrs. Maier said when my dad came, show-and-tell could continue again. I told her I'd keep waiting. On the playground during recess, I waited. I told the kids that my Papi was still coming—"Just wait."

Mrs. Maier asked if I wanted to call my dad during nap time because I couldn't go to sleep. I told her I couldn't nap because my dad was coming. I didn't want to miss him. But I didn't know his phone numbers. Not for the black phone or the blue phone or any phone.

Mrs. Maier said I could just lay down and not close my eyes. Then the tingles in my throat came back, stronger than before. They moved inside my mouth and were in my eyes. I was stuck lying, looking at the back of Krista's sandy blonde hair. I didn't know what time it was. I didn't know why my Papi wasn't there, but I knew he was still coming.

He said so.

He promised.

I started crying.

* * *

I woke up to Mrs. Maier clinking bell chimes. I knew it was almost time to go home. I stayed quiet until the school bell rang. I waited in front of my classroom door to go home. Krista's dad picked her up before me, and I had to wait again, longer.

"You missed show-and-tell," I yelled to my Papi as soon as I saw him. I kept my hands tight on my backpack straps that day and didn't let go when he held out his hand.

"Agh, I forgot," my Papi said in the car. I didn't put on the radio—only my seat belt. I think he kept talking, but all I can remember is he *forgot*.

And then I remember crying so hard, I couldn't say any words. I am certain he said he was sorry. I am certain he probably told me not to cry in that booming tone my Mami said was *just his voice*. I am certain I kept crying.

I did not want to lose show-and-tell. I wanted to prove to Mrs. Maier and my classmates that they were wrong—my Papi would come. My Papi promised. Promises are supposed to be forever and ever, and dads aren't supposed to lie. But I could feel the point when my classmates didn't believe me, and eventually when Mrs. Maier stopped believing too. I hated the feeling of not being believed when I still believed in my Papi. *My Papi promised*. Promises are supposed to be forever and ever, and dads aren't supposed to lie. I needed to believe my Papi could keep his word and never forget me. I still wish I could believe.

02. heartbreak hotel

"Talk to me!" was my favorite way to answer the phone when I was six years old. I heard my cousin Amanda say it first and it was so cool I had to try. I had only tested it out about three times total before my Mami said I wouldn't be allowed to answer the phone if I kept doing it—*dumb*! Answering the phone was the best and so even though "talk to me" was the best too, I didn't want to be banned from picking up the telephone for the rest of my life. I switched back to plain ol' "hello." Maybe because Mami was now 30, old and "over the hill" according to the balloons she got, she would become stricter?

Our townhouse in Belmont looked two stories tall from the outside and had two phones on the inside. It was built on a hill and looked kind of like a cookie—cream with brown pieces of wood crisscrossed in a style my Mami said was English Tudor, even though we lived in the United States. Inside, our family lived on the upstairs floor because all that could fit downstairs was a garage. Whenever someone called, the phone would ring through our whole house with the curly-Q corded phone in my Mami and Papi's room going off first and the fancy cordless phone in the kitchen catching up a few seconds later.

I would stop whatever I was doing every time I heard the trill and run to the phone that was closest. My mission was always to beat my sister and luckily, we got phone calls all the time. Sometimes from my cousins Monica and Amanda, or their mom, Tia Silvia. Sometimes it was Tia Sylvia, or even Papi. Occasionally it was just solicitors. I loved the surprise of not knowing who might be on the other end.

But, a couple weeks after my littlest brother Hector's third birthday, we got a phone call that was like no others before. I picked up the phone in the kitchen and said "Hello." There was a lady on the other side whose voice I didn't recognize (yet). She said she needed to speak to Maria.

"Moooooooom," I yelled from the kitchen. "Telephone! It's for you."

I told the lady to hold on. Then, we both waited without talking. I think maybe I tried to listen for her breath or any clues to uncover who this mystery woman could be—I was always nosy like that, but I got nothing. My mom told me to always ask who was calling, but this time I forgot. I didn't know who was on the other side of the line when my Mami asked. She picked up the phone from her room a few seconds later and told me to hang up. My sister swears, in adulthood, she was the one to pick up—the child to wonder who was on the line. When we ask our Mami for the truth, this part of the memory has blurred too much for her too. But we all agree on what came next.

I went back to what I was doing—probably watching Nickelodeon with Hector in the living room or playing with my Barbies—and got sucked in for a long time in that way where everything would disappear and all that could snap me out of my trance was a commercial break or someone yelling. I remembered hearing the murmurs of Erika talking to Mami down the hallway and being curious but unable to hear what about. I walked away from the living room, past the kitchen and dining room table and the hallway bathroom, toward their voices. At the end of the hall, I saw Erika's and my room was mysteriously empty— TV, lights, and all, still on. The white bedroom door right across from ours—Mami's and Papi's—wasn't all the way shut. I pushed it open.

Mami and Erika were both laying on the bed together, on top of the sábanas, crying hard. My Mami couldn't look at me. She just wiped the wet of her cheeks, tears silently streaming, without saying a word. Erika's face was buried into Mami's chest.

"What's wrong?" my small voice asked.

I had never seen Mami cry before. She was always so strong. *What could be happening?* They both kept crying, which only made me more scared. *Why wouldn't they answer me? Why wouldn't they talk?*

I asked again, nervously, already starting to feel my crying coming.

"Your Papi's not going to live with us anymore," my Mami said.

I froze, the pool of tears filling the bottom of my eyes. My forehead felt hot. I knew if I blinked the water would pour and I wouldn't be able to stop it.

"What do you mean?" I tried again. "Why?"

"The lady who called said PAPI'S NOT COMING HOME," yelled Erika.

I kept listening, but they didn't say anymore. My Mami just kept her eyes closed and kept crying with my sister. The breath in my chest started to get shaky. I let out my tears, crying out loud and hard too. Everything was hot and blurry. I crawled into my Mami and Papi's bed. I hugged my Mami and sister both tight. We all cried together.

* * *

That night, and every night for a whole week, my sister and I slept on a tendido on my Mami's bedroom floor. She helped us lay down a big gray quilted bufanda that felt like a windbreaker and our favorite Las Pulgas blankets—a ferocious black-and-white fleece tiger, bootleg blonde-haired Belle from *Beauty and the Beast*, and the one with the green-and-black rose. Mami slept in the bed with Hector. Erika stayed home from middle school and I stayed home from my elementary. Mami stayed home from work. We kept crying together.

I wondered why my Papi wasn't coming home. *Why did the lady call to tell my Mami? Why didn't Papi call me or tell me first? Why didn't he want to live with me? I thought he loved me.*

Every way I asked her, Mami just said he wasn't coming back. I didn't understand why, but I understood this was forever. He wasn't going to be our Papi—at least not like the other kids' dads were, living together in one big house like a happy family.

After our week of saying goodbye to Papi, I still felt just as sad, but sometimes during the day I would forget my sadness. I would feel like everything was normal, until something reminded me of my Papi, or of dads. And I would always remember at night. When my Mami fell asleep hugging toddler Hector tight in her arms, Erika hugged me every night too. Even though Erika said she hated me, she had always forced me to be a little spoon since forever, since even before Papi left. I think the week Papi left she hugged me extra tight, and I know she definitely did after he was gone. When the house was dark and quiet, when me and my sister were alone together in our room, I would remember our Papi wasn't there. But I would remember Mami and Erika and Hector were.

* * *

It was 1998 when Mami had her first Mother's Day with just her kids and Abuelita—no man. A few weeks after that, we went to our first family party since our own familia had been severed.

I was playing with my cousins in the shade of a palm tree. We were in the front yard of the first house we ever lived in as a family—a Fair Oaks cul-de-sac bordering East Menlo. I could see the screen door and front door where my crazed Papi had caught me picking my nose and eating my boogers—not once but twice within minutes when I could barely speak full sentences. Just beyond that, I could see the brown carpet of the living room where I first learned to walk.

Under my old favorite palm, my prima Iselita told me my Papi had a new happy family. She said he already had a brand-new everything—including a baby.

I told my prima Iselita she was lying. My prima Iselita told me she was not.

Then she held up a picture of a round, pale baby with brown curls and squishy cheeks. I looked at the picture. I looked into the eyes of the cherub—my new perfect sister—and then into the eyes of my prima Iselita. I told her she was lying.

I had always liked babies. I had always liked looking at baby pictures. But this cute baby picture made me feel too many damn things at once. I was sad and mad and embarrassed and confused. So, I pretended I didn't want to look at the baby picture anymore, even though I wanted to snatch it and maybe keep it safe forever, or maybe rip it apart.

I didn't tell my Mami I had a new baby sister in Chicago. Now I think she probably already knew.

03. amor prohibido

In THIRD GRADE my hobbies are playing soccer, watching Rugrats, and crushing on boys. My boy crushes flip back-and-forth between David and Connor. I also love Justin Timberlake, but sometimes JC Chasez too.

David is a tall third-grader who is half Filipino with thick black hair, just like mine. Connor is a cool, blue-eyed white boy with dirty blonde hair. His skin seems to be sun-kissed every day of the year, but especially after summers on Southern California beaches where he says his family goes to surf. Neither of these boys like me back, but that doesn't stop me from dreaming of the day they will.

Although my Mami can leave work on time to pick me up at the last bell, I ask her to come later so I can hang out with the *popular* kids at after-school care. I want to be a popular kid. I want to fit in—feel like I'm normal and pretty. I like wearing Gap sweatshirts and three stripe Adidas shoes like the other kids. I only like speaking English now too. But I don't look like them, and they tell me with their eyes my skin is brown and tell me with their words my nose is big. Later, in middle school, they will learn to yell out "honk honk!" as a shorthand. Even later, when I am in high school, I will beg my parents for plastic surgery as my graduation gift—a normal request in Belmont, California—and they will agree. But before I graduate, I will drop the idea, having learned not to care quite so much about my *honker*.

When my sister, Erika, was still at our elementary school, she and I and maybe three other kids were Mexican. By third grade, I think only three of us are left. But I don't care about finding other brown kids to hang out with. I prefer after-care where I get more time to hang out with Connor and David and my pretty blonde haired, blue-eyed best friend, Krista. I have more time to get them all to like me. Plus, at after-care, there are also snacks, which I eat a bunch of, but not *too much* when the boys are around. We all eat chips, and I already know it would be weird if I ever dared to eat more than one bag of chips—even weirder if I ate more than the *growing boys*.

One day at after-care, I race to the glider as soon I can, stomping all over the wood chips. The glider is the coolest place to be on the playground. On this day, there is only one boy swinging when I get there. During the school day, the line is usually six kids deep—*score!*

The way the glider works is that you hold your body up by squeezing a green, horseshoe-shaped piece of metal real tight with one or two hands. Then, while holding the piece of metal, you drift down along a track. If you're any good, you know a running start provides maximum momentum, giving you enough power to swing back to the starting point without stopping. If you are bad, you can't even hold yourself up. I'm so good, I can swing with just one arm.

I laze on the dark gridded platform to wait for my turn. Waiting behind one person is nothing. Connor walks up behind me with his best friend, Taylor. Taylor has auburn hair and really pale skin that looks like a glass of two percent. Rowan, a skinny bucktoothed white boy who looks like and talks like Bart Simpson, follows. I swear to God, Rowan is obsessed with being a follower, but even more obsessed with bullying (me). I hate him so much.

The four of us wait for Victor, the quiet Greek boy one grade younger than us, as he swings his body along the glider. He is small and has to stop a few times. Feeling generous, I give him a few extra turns. Connor asks if I am having fun waiting for my *boyfriend* to stop swinging and the boys—except Victor—start to laugh.

"He's not my boyfriend," I say, annoyed that my crush Conner would even think I was crushing on anyone other than him (or David.)

"That *second* grader is not my boyfriend," I say, louder, again, as they keep laughing.

The tingling in my throat that loves to grip on tight, making it hard to swallow, spreads—my familiar disease. I feel my heart starting to pound, up and down, heavy. Eventually, the boys stop laughing. Victor swings back and plops down next to me on the grid. It's finally my time to take a swing.

I get ready for my mighty run by pulling up my bell bottoms. I make sure the glider is right near the starting point of the track, but a few inches away from touching the edge. This makes it easier to jump on and keep sliding without slowing down.

The sun is bright, but the air is cold and windy, so I am ready to warm up and move around. Just as I back away to leap into my sprint, Rowan announces there is no way Victor could ever be my boyfriend.

I put my fingers back through the loops of my pants, pretending I need further adjusting, and wait, intrigued. Connor, my crush, asks Rowan why. Then time stands still.

It's like creepy Rowan waved a pocket watch and hypnotized us all. We stare at Rowan's mouth, waiting for the words to come out, probably with a signature touch of spit. Then Rowan takes a dramatic, deep breath and looks me right in the eyes. He fails to hold back his maniacal smile.

"He can't be her boyfriend because—he'd have to paint his skin *black*!" Rowan yells.

I freeze.

I look to Connor.

Connor almost seems frozen too. And then he lets out a huge, hearty laugh. And the boys—except Victor—are cracking up too.

I run straight ahead. I grasp at the glider handle, snapping my legs harder than I ever have to make sure I can make the return. A bang so-loud-it-hurts rings out as I reach the end of the track, metal hitting metal. My fingers loosen for a second, and then I grip harder.

The first tears fall down my face. I think my cheeks are on fire. In seconds, I'm back at the start without an escape plan. I try to think of all the bad words I can yell out and all the ways to tell them they are wrong. Instead, I can't get my words or think straight. I bawl and hyperventilate my way back to the after-care building without looking back.

I sit in the lap of the white after-school-care lady and she hugs me while I wait for my Mami to pick me up. The after-school-care lady is so pretty and cool, with chunky highlights and a half pony on the top of her head sticking out of her clear visor. I know she is being as nice as she possibly can to me. I also know she doesn't really understand.

The nice after-care lady tells me she talked to Rowan and told him what he said wasn't nice. She tells my mom what happened too. And that is that.

People call me names at school, like ugly, and I believe them. I am not beautiful like Britney Spears. Sometimes my classmates say that me and my "big honking nose" should go back to Mexico. But this is the first time someone called me *too dark*. So loud, and so clear. I remember thinking I could have said "I am Mexican, not Black" but I also knew in that moment it didn't even matter. The point was I am too different—my skin is too dark—and I will never be liked by someone who isn't dark like me too. So, I think this all means I am doomed. No one will ever like me back—at least not in vanilla white Belmont, California.

04. super nova girl

THE CERULEAN GLOW of the square television set illuminates my bedroom as it hangs above the dresser. It's Friday night. I am 10 years old. I *live* for Disney Channel Original Movies, and *Zenon: The Zequel* is debuting.

While the opening credits roll, I walk into the kitchen, past my mom and Hector, to grab the wrinkled white paper bag. *Courage the Cowardly Dog* is on and my mom uses two-thirds of the kitchen table to fold our laundry. Erika is out at a football game again and won't be home until late. I wonder if her friend, Anne, has found the band-aid I stuck into her poofy brown hair yet—the one I put on right before we dropped them off at the Serra High School football game.

I place the Wendy's bag on top of a TV tray positioned right in the middle of my room. The milky rubber chair I picked out from the Target dorm room collection to make me feel older fits perfectly behind it. I close my Spice Girl sticker-laden door for privacy and to block out the sound of cartoons from my baby brother.

As I unload the bag, I carefully fold the sack for recycling. The soda cup holding my Dr. Pepper is covered in tiny beads of water. I wipe them away with a napkin. I peel the waxed wrapper to reveal a melty, square junior bacon cheeseburger. Its sesame bun is generously seeded and crisped to perfection. I release the salty fries from their packaging onto the wrapper and, next to it, deposit two mounds of cherry-red ketchup.

Finally, the movie begins. A blonde pigtailed white girl in pink and blue latex squeals: "The first rock concert is coming to space!"

I take my first bite of burger and think: *This is the best Friday night ever.*

I am happy.

05. tragos amargos

WHEN I WAS ten years old, I spent an entire month in the town where you were raised. Aguililla was a mountainous place where I came to know a new meaning of what it meant to be free—where I got a glimpse of what growing up for you, Papi, might have felt like. Burros and horses clacked their hooves on the cobblestone roads in *Little Eagle*. Young callejeros zipped through the streets stacked on bikes, in truck beds, piled high atop ATVs, boy bodies pressed, hands gripping legs, metal, arms, to hold on. People came far and wide across town, cycled in and out of the heavy wooden front door, through the house back to the kitchen in search of queso freshly-pressed by Coyo's hands using milk Papa Nano tugged from their vacas' utters. Clean water was delivered, by the pila, once a week.

In Aguililla, the sister city to the Madera Roja where I was born, there were other little brown girls like me. There, aside from that chiquillo, Carlingas, the kids mostly seemed to treat me as their equals—I passed as normal with ease. There, my Spanish still came to me with fluidity and familiarity—not yet plagued by the fear of sounding too American, too pochita. Not yet entangled in the complexity of what it means to be Chicana, split in two, or to be your daughter, split in many.

When I was ten, I spent the longest stretch of time with you without knowing it would be the longest stretch of my life. Allí en Aguililla, I became captivated by our Mexican history and of your past life as a vaquero. I imagined you might have liked spiraling down the slide at the public pool, arms crossed, into crisp jade water as a kid with me, "Ciega, Sordomudo" blaring. I could see us playing soccer in the street together with the other kids, gladly getting soaked by the warm rainstorms even when we knew it meant trouble. There in Aguililla, I learned to dress myself in the same nationalistic pride and leather huaraches as the ones you adorned yourself with. There, in our own little ranch, I christened the pregnant cow you let me pick out as my own with the name of Ángel—for the confidence I still had in God and in you as a father. Todavía no supé que en el futuro I'd come to doubt both after spending months without hearing a word from either. Todavía sin comprender que en el futuro the cows, too, would come to lose their sparkle—the cows a veil for the truth, the cows too, victims of your web of lies.

* * *

When I was ten, I found myself in the midst of the cycle my life was destined to repeat. A cycle marred by growing up unjustly fast. A cycle as excessively accelerated and rebellious as the torrential downpour so common in your hometown. A cycle we'd both come to share.

There in Aguililla, I came to know the type of leisure that formed your youth—the sense of safety, of roaming until dark, of being on your own. Rosa taught me lime wedges were multifunctional—suitable to mask the taste of tequila even to a 10-year-old, or to lighten the strands of my brown hair to blonde, or maybe even lighten my mahogany knees. The sixteen-

year-old country boy taught me how I could be kissed, taught me
that I could still be destined to be kissed by more than just the
girls I'd kissed in kindergarten and maybe could still be normal.
That sixteen-year-old boy taught me my ten-year-old little girl
boobs could be caressed, that my body could be desired in this
way by men. That the boys my age didn't like me because they
were immature. I also learned that at my novio's side I became
branded: my childish body was suddenly protected against the
catcalls and whistles of viejos rabos verdes when on the arm of
a male.

When I was ten, I hadn't yet formed the walls of stone you
helped me build. I was still without the ganas I'd come to gain
on my own—product of my own strength, shaped by the women
around me. I also never suspected that you, Papi, would be the
most complicated puzzle of my life. I could have never suspected
that at 25 I'd continue my investigation of our country anew. I'd
return for another month to Michoacán still in search of clues.
Still in search of things to uncover—and reveal—your secrets.
Simple answers to help pinpoint when and why our relationship
became rotten. Still hoping to help you unearth the emotions
you left buried here in the campo. Returning to nuestro rancho,
begging the cows to forgive you—pleading that they, too, excuse
you for your prolonged absences.

Here in Aguililla, tracing the tracks of our homeland,
searching for the innocence we both lost. Here in the United
States, hoping to bandage my wounds instead of inheriting our
family's brokenness. Here at home, waiting for the moment
you'll realize our memories will never fade. Here, wishing that
one day you'll also return, Papi, to free yourself from the past.
Here, still wishing we might have a future. Here, still wishing to
be fathered.

06. keep ya head up

I DON'T REMEMBER when I stopped praying to God to make me white. I had stopped lacing my fingers at the side of my bed nightly, hoping I'd wake up with blue eyes and blonde hair, long before I stopped the whisper-praying to God in my head for the same want.

For a while, I tried coating strands of my hair in lime juice and scrubbing my knees with lime halves until they were rubbed raw, like how Rosa from Aguililla taught me. I believed her when she said they would make me lighter, even though Rosa's eyes and hair and skin were still darker than mine. I figured it just took time and *patience*. I wanted to believe her, and I wanted to believe in God too. I thought, *He wouldn't mind if I used all-natural ways to speed up the process—if I used the Earth to make me look less like Her.*

I just wanted to feel like I belonged.

* * *

When I got to Newton Middle School in sixth grade, I was tired of trying to fit in. *If I am going to be treated differently by kids and parents and teachers, I might as well look and act differently. I'm not fooling anyone pretending I am just like everyone else.*

My first experiment in being loudly different was going punk.

I picked out a black Ramones t-shirt from Mervyn's and a necklace made up of silver metal balls during Back-to-School shopping with my mom. Hot Topic had the perfect cool belt: red pleather with silver studs. Macy's had a less punk selection, but I found a red DKNY tank top that had buildings and a sassy slit down the front.

My mom wouldn't let me dye my hair red for picture day, so I poured on the Sun-In Spray in the bathroom. Erika had tried using Sun-In to get "auburn" hair but turned it orangey-brown instead. She went to a real hairdresser after that. I figured the rest of the bottle and orange-colored hair was good enough for me.

After I got my Ramones shirt, I downloaded their music from the Internet with Napster. It took forever to download—like two hours—but I got a couple of songs and listened to them on repeat: "Beat on the Brat" and "I Wanna Be Sedated" were my favorite. I was kinda surprised punk wasn't as loud and fast as I thought it was supposed to be. I wanted things I could shout with when I wanted to scream, which was often. I found some other punk music that was louder and faster and angrier, just like me.

I changed my AIM screen name to LinkinPark41—dedicated 50 percent to Linkin Park and 50 percent to Sum 41. Avril Lavigne was also really cool, so I bought her CD. I loved listening to her slow, shouty songs—not the ones on the radio—and I'd blast them from my red, bubble-shaped boom box when I took showers. I thought it was cool to call these pain-laced screaming tracks "underground" because they weren't on the radio, even though they were on a major label. I always wanted to be the one in the know, *discovering* tracks before they were on MTV's *TRL* or better yet, BET's *106 & Park*.

There weren't very many punk kids at Newton, but the ones I did see didn't look like me and weren't cool with me. I thought I had totally convinced my Latina friend, Monique, to go punk with me because she said yes but then she chickened out before picture day. She was such a poser. I, on the other hand, begged my mom to pay extra so I could get a red background for picture day. I looked very punk.

I liked punk music and the fashion, but there weren't enough punk kids I could actually hang out with. I didn't want to be a poser, hanging out with only preppy kids, so I slowly stopped being punk. My mom was hella mad because I asked her to spend $50 on a black Dickie's jacket and stopped being punk a week later. I felt kinda guilty, but when I was preppy again for a while, I just couldn't wear stuff like that anymore. I don't know why she didn't get that.

Not long after, I began experimenting with being a chola. It came easy. I already had a lot of red clothing from being punk. Rap, R&B, and oldies were in rotation on the soundtrack of my upbringing, along with Spanish-language cumbias, pop, and even rock. My mom was even a homegirl back in the day, rocking feathered hair and Pachuca style. My Uncle Baby still talked like a cholo. Being chola was a birthright. It was in my blood.

I changed my AIM screen name to GhettoMexican650 and made an AOL email this time to match. I was going to be chola forever.

Although Belmont was hella white, Newton Middle School, unlike Garibaldi Elementary School, had Black and brown kids who looked like me. Most of them came on buses from East Palo Alto and Redwood Shores, but I learned that a few of them lived in Belmont too, just on the other side. For the first time in my life, there were other people I could hang out with like me—people who weren't white and who also didn't quite fit in because of the color of their skin.

* * *

Being a chola started out fun. I felt beautiful and badass with gel-slicked hair hard against my forehead, curls nice and crunchy—looking permanently wet—with extra firm hair spray. With my Baby Phat jeans and straight-laced Chucks. I felt strong, too. Bitches were suddenly even more scared to talk shit to me. I talked back to teachers now too. I became a pro at shooting people dirty-ass looks to make them feel disgusting. I loved rolling my eyes, all dramatic, right in front of peoples' faces. I had new friends who other people were afraid of too.

I don't know what happened first—being chola or being bad at school—but it all seemed to happen at once. I hadn't *loved* school since first grade, but I started to hate school. All teachers cared about was telling us what to do. They made us do dumb-ass projects I didn't care about. Everything sucked. Why should I care about ancient Rome or the layers of the earth? Why should I have to read dusty, boring textbooks or *The Hobbit*, some garbage make-believe magic book about hairy little men with weird feet?

Nothing at school was interesting to me. It all felt fake—nothing like what real people like me dealt with every day. I didn't have anything in common with people from Mesopotamia! Plus, so many preppy kids talked about having crazy good GPAs like 3.8's and 4.0's. I had to try pretty hard to get a 3.2 GPA. I couldn't even imagine how I'd ever get much higher than that. But it seemed so easy for my rich preppy friends, and I felt like an idiot. Why should I even keep trying if I'd never be that smart?

When parent-teacher conferences rolled around at the end of the first trimester, the results were a slap in the face to my mom. I had always done okay in school—Bs mostly—but she found out I barely had a 2.0 with mostly Cs and Ds.

She cried in front of my teachers as they told her how bad I was doing; how bad I was. I had only seen her cry once before in front of me—after that phone call when we learned my dad was leaving our family for Camy and their new family—and here she was, crying in front of me and strangers. I just sat there while they talked about me, in front of me, like I was invisible. I was mad that my mom was crying. I told her Ds were technically passing grades. I lied that I'd try to do better.

Pretty soon, I felt like I was always in trouble at school and always in a fight with someone. At home, my sister Erika and my mom were always fighting with me. Hector was annoying and just sat around playing video games, too. My mom said I had an "attitude problem." It was her favorite thing to say. I also supposedly had "anger problems." My dad only seemed to want to talk to me when my mom told me I was in trouble. He only ever called my phone to yell at me. Never called to ask how I was doing or made an effort to go to my soccer games. Things with my dad—or anyone for that matter—weren't very good.

* * *

I had been really close with my stepmom, Camy, growing up. My mom and my dad talked on the phone every week and both said they wanted us all to have a good relationship. My mom was really supportive of me being close with Camy. There was only this one time—when I found pictures of me and Camy hugging at the Guadalajara zoo, taped shut in an envelope and shoved into the kitchen junk drawer—that I ever thought it might make my mom feel weird. But my mom never said anything. I liked talking to Camy and I think my mom liked that I had someone to talk to.

Camy understood my dad because she lived with him. She was always listening to what I had to say. She encouraged me a lot, unlike most adults I knew, and tried to help me accomplish my dreams. On one visit to Texas, where she grew up, Camy styled me and did my makeup when I told her I wanted to be a model. She told me I looked beautiful and should have self-confidence. We straightened my hair, and I wore a black rhinestone Bebe t-shirt, jeans, and strappy heels. She took photos of me posing, smiling, and we mailed them to an ad we saw in the back of a magazine looking for models. She helped me like this because I told her being a model was my dream. She also bought me a disposable camera and really pretty picture albums when I told her I wanted to be a photographer. She taught me how to take a nice photo—how to look through the little square and make sure I captured the beauty of the world at the right angle.

We'd gotten to know each other pretty well over the years and when I was 13, I thought we'd have a good relationship forever. But we got into a huge fight one day. It felt out of the blue, but we both couldn't let it go. She was mad at me for something I said when I was like 10 years old, but also for not keeping in touch. I didn't get why she was bringing it up—the thing that happened when I was ten, three years later—but I didn't want to keep saying sorry to her. I thought it was such an empty thing to still be mad about.

What happened when I was ten was that I was in Texas visiting her, my dad, and my little sisters, Pao and Vivi. We were all there together, visiting Camy's parents. I loved going to that town outside of Houston to swim, ride ATVs, and race go-karts. I also loved spending time with my family.

This song I had never heard before came on the radio while just me and Camy were driving one night. It's called "Life Goes On" by Leann Rimes. The lyrics reminded me of my mom and dad:

> *Baby, shame on you if you fool me once.*
> *Shame on me if you fool me twice.*
> *You've been a pretty hard case to crack.*
> *Should've known better*
> *But I didn't*
> *And I can't go back.*
> *Oh, life goes on.*
> *And it's only gonna make me strong.*

So, I blurted out, "This song is like my mom with my dad!"

I think she asked me what I meant, and I had to explain that 'fool me once' was like when Papi cheated on my Mami with

Paloma (my sister Daniela and brother Hector Jr.'s mom). 'Fool me twice' and the rest was like when Papi cheated on Mami with Camy and how that was the last straw—it was hard for my Mami, but life goes on and she got through it.

I don't remember her seeming mad or sad or anything after, but I had to apologize to Camy on the phone after the trip to Texas. I thought she'd get over it, but then she'd bring it up what felt like every few months. I'd have to apologize to her over and over and sometimes she'd accept it, but sometimes she wouldn't.

I felt bad for hurting her feelings, but I felt like I was just telling the truth. I thought lying was always bad, and I thought omitting parts of the truth were just as bad as lies. I also thought we were close. I thought she knew how much I loved her, still. But I also felt my dad would take her side, and I thought he'd always take his new family's side. I didn't know why both my dad and Camy only expected me to do the calling, the staying in touch and maintaining *our relationship*. By the end of sixth grade, I didn't want to keep begging him or her to be on my side. I stopped talking much to either of them.

* * *

At school, there was always drama. Monique had become my enemy again (we were always best friends and then enemies and then friends—true *frenemies*). Though I was friends with Jessica, Heidi, Krista, and Michelle, I often still felt hella lonely. I never had a solid crew like some of the other girls. I wanted a clique that was big and that stuck together.

But my friends were always changing. My grades were tanking. I hated being at home. I hated being at school. Sometimes I had a boyfriend, but nothing felt for real. It would only last like a week or three tops. Everything was changing, and it felt like it was changing for the worse.

I started to see therapists who were supposed to help me feel better. I didn't trust any of them. They were all white and old. How would they ever understand what it was like to be me? I tried to say as little as possible.

One old man therapist called for an open family conversation when I told him me and my sister had gotten into a fist-fight in the kitchen one day. I had been proud that I got a few swings in on her since she's five years older than me, and he repeated the story, minus the proud part, to my mom. He said he could've reported this to Child Protective Services, but he chose to have the conversation with my mom instead. I thought he was such a fucking snitch. He was dead to me.

Another therapist, a white lady with dark brown curls, also pulled my mom into a conversation once but with my permission. She told my mom I was suffering from depression. The therapist said there were meds that could help me feel better, but in the car on the drive home my mom warned me that I might get hooked and depend on meds for the rest of my life. She said it was my choice. I was scared. I didn't want to get addicted to anything. I didn't want to depend on anyone or anything. I wanted to be strong on my own.

I don't know when exactly, but I started to try "cutting." I heard other kids who suffered from depression did it to help them feel better. I didn't like blood and I didn't know how cutting myself could make me feel better, but I figured I would try. I didn't tell any therapists.

I thought about killing myself before. I thought about how I might kill myself. I could never shoot myself or hang myself. Those were too messy and hard. I was afraid of drowning in the ocean or burning my body in a fire. But falling asleep and never waking up after taking pills seemed easy. The problem was, I was just too scared to actually do it.

Honestly though, I didn't really want to die. Dying was scary. Thinking about the nothingness of what being dead must feel like, the blankness that I knew probably happened to us instead of some kind of heaven, terrified me. But I just didn't want to feel all this pain, sadness, emptiness, and hate all the time. I was tired of feeling like I was failing at everything, like I was dumb, ugly, and worthless. And if I died, at least I wouldn't have to keep feeling like this every day. I imagined my funeral and how everyone would pretend like they had been my friend. How my fake friends and family members would want to speak about how I'd died too young, was gone too soon. How maybe then, people would start to care about me and talk about me like they liked me. How people would miss me and wish I were around.

I heard the real way to die was cutting vertically so your slice could travel the length of a vein and have more impact. I decided to cut horizontally on my wrist and on my leg. I used a dull pair of scissors a few times so it would hurt but I wouldn't die. It was hard to push the blade in and I had to keep rubbing it until the skin broke. Eventually, I made blood come out and did it a few more times.

Kids at school the next day kept asking me if I was okay. The attention felt nice, but the cutting didn't really make me feel better. Instead, I spent a lot of time alone and listening to music.

* * *

Through all the changes, I had music. Music was there for me when people weren't.

Tupac Amaru Shakur was my real teacher—*fuck school*. Tupac taught me about the world. He taught me about what real people go through and live through every day. He taught me about poverty, corrupt police, and racism. He taught me what the United States is really like. How this country wasn't built to love Black or brown people. He taught me my skin is beautiful.

He was the first person to tell me how lucky I am to be brown. He taught me *I* was beautiful.

Whenever I was feeling especially sad, I'd pop on "Keep Ya Head Up" to remind myself I was beautiful. I'd close my eyes, cry, and listen to every word on repeat:

> *Some say the blacker the berry, the sweeter the juice*
> *I say the darker the flesh, then the deeper the roots*
> *I give a holler to my sisters on welfare*
> *Tupac cares, if don't nobody else care*
> *And uh, I know they like to beat ya down a lot*
> *When you come around the block brothas clown a lot*
> *But please don't cry, dry your eyes, never let up*
> *Forgive but don't forget, girl keep your head up*

Tupac didn't really know his dad and, although he was often mad at his mom, he loved her—just like me. People judged Tupac for what he looked like and sounded like. All people saw when they saw Tupac was his anger. They didn't know just how damn smart he was. They didn't take the time to listen to his words and listen to what he had to say. Tupac had been suicidal but survived. Tupac was misunderstood. Tupac was just like me.

If Tupac could believe in himself and people like him, even when the world seemed to be against him and everyone else Black and brown, I figured I should learn how to also.

When Tupac says he cares, I believe him. I know he's speaking to me and wants me to be safe. I think I owe it to him to try and keep my head up, especially when so many people have harder lives and still have the strength to live on. I sometimes think God may have forgotten about helping me, like everyone else, but I know Tupac didn't. He saved my life. He taught me I am beautiful.

* * *

For the rest of sixth and seventh grade, I will continue to struggle with my grades, my attitude, and my depression. I'll spend the first half of eighth grade doing really well, getting passing grades and staying out of trouble because my teachers tell me and my mom I might be held back and stay in middle school if I continue down my flunky academic trajectory. The longing to leave Newton forever and to attend a special eighth grade trip to New York City (*tight*) and Washington D.C. (*boring*) become the fire I need to stay on track. Any student who has the money can attend this trip across the country, so long as they don't get more than three detentions in one year. I make a pact with my mother that if I get good grades I can go on the trip *and* attend a high school in Redwood City, not in white ass Belmont. I think she'll try just about anything if it means I don't fail out of school.

For the first half of eight grade, I remain on track. I manage to keep my detention tally down to one—far fewer than the fifty-plus I racked up the year prior. I'm still severely depressed, but on paper, my report card says I am doing well. When I tear my ACL in a soccer game and wind up on crutches for three months, I take this as a sign God is listening: I prayed for an injury—a broken arm—so people would show me they cared, and he delivers. I am appointed gym teacher aide which mostly means I sit in a warm office while my classmates jog outside. Two other friends become T.A.s too. Sometimes we take pictures of each other on my sister's digital camera. Other days we push each other around on spinny chairs. It's while sitting around one day bored stiff—only a couple years after *Jackass: The Movie* and *The Ring* came out—that we decide a spooky school prank would be hilarious. So, we use the Xerox machine to photocopy our faces and hands and, surprisingly, no butts. We crack up as we see our creations and learn that moving hair and limbs across the translucent plate, mid-scan, makes for creepier copies. Another classmate throws in some middle fingers. It becomes a competition at whose can be the scariest, and we get high from the sheer thrill. We print off a bunch of our unique creations, then stuff them into different student lockers before the next period lets out.

When I am pulled into the vice principal's office later that day, or maybe that week, I am greeted by the familiar face of the 30-something white guy who acts as the school's heavy. I have come to know this office and his face well due to my many instances of *too short skirts, too much cleavage,* or *inappropriately* sitting through the Pledge of Allegiance in protest. He's sitting there, copies splayed, behind his desk. He tells me they figured out I am guilty—I'm the only student who had access to a copy machine at that hour. I tell him all I wanted was a fun eighth grade school prank—*hadn't he heard of the epic San Mateo County high school shenanigans of Senior Week?*

The vice principal asks me who else was involved. I say I don't want to get anyone in trouble.

He plays "Juicy" by The Notorious B.I.G. and says he loves old school hip-hop *too*. I try to keep my head from bobbing to the bass.

"Biggie may have had the beats on lock, but Pac always kills it with his lyrics," I say. "Plus, West Side represent."

The vice principal picks out a black-and-white prank page from his desk and smooths it out before pointing to something a lighter shade of gray, something angled. He turns *Ready to Die* down low. He says he doesn't care too much about the middle fingers but asks me what's in the center of those shadows. I tell him they're probably just fast-moving fingers. Then he accuses us of brandishing a knife.

"That's not a knife!" I sputter.

He says we scared students.

"It was just a *joke*," I try to explain.

The vice principal says he knows I didn't act alone. He wants to know who else was involved. He says he knows I don't want to get in trouble. He says it would be a huge help if I told him— they'd definitely be able to figure it out on their own, but if I tell him, it will speed things up and save everyone time.

The vice principal is using *lingo*, talking like eighth grade me. He's saying thing likes "It's coo'" and is leaning back in his chair like this is all casual. Biggie is still on in the background. He says he knows how much I've turned things around this year, and that he'll keep that in mind—and my help—when it comes to *the consequences.*

"I'm going to ask you one more time," he says. "Who else helped you out?"

And that is how the vice principal convinces me to rat out my two friends.

I am suspended from school for the first time in my academic career. My suspension sentence is one day. My Mami believes me when I tell her in the car, sobbing, that the vice principal said he'd let me off easier if I snitched. I tell her I didn't want to tell him—and that he still suspended me. She tries to plead with the principal for a detention instead so I can still go on the eighth-grade trip. She points out the manipulation but the vice principal says he never promised me a thing. The principal says he doesn't have the power to redact a suspension.

I can barely look at my friends when I am at school two days later. I don't remember their sentences, but I think I might have been the only one suspended; violation of my T.A. privileges.

I don't get to go to New York City or a Redwood City high school, or even Washington D.C. I'll get high and get drunk for the first time, in the same week, later on in the semester. My grades start to slip. I vow to never be a snitch again.

07. so rich, so pretty

I BEGIN STARVING myself by accident.

The allure of being seen as a pit bull has mostly waned when my Mami promises high school might just be the perfect time to reinvent myself.

There is a self-assuredness that comes with knowing I could get scrappy and chunk it—handle my own—at least with any white girl at my school, and I am afraid to lose that. But it has started to feel like digging deeper into the ways I am different from all these white people only makes things worse. After spending most of my middle school years listening to the realest Bay Area Norteño rap on repeat—Darkroom Familia and Woodie spitting about Califas were my favorite—and gelling my copéte down, and wishing I was a real Norteña, my gut knows I'm scared of what it would mean to be truly jumped in, even though I would never admit it aloud. I know that I will never be down enough to want this life forever. I remain loud and brown enough to scare most people around me, but not tight enough to hang with the cholas outside of school. And so, I decide to return to the in-between, even though I have really always been here. I still feel mostly alone.

I decide starting fresh, like a Cady Heron transfer, sounds real nice. If blending in is what it takes to avoid that look people give you when they assume you are only going to fail now and forever, well, then, I am in.

I am fourteen years old and five-foot-two.

* * *

When I start high school, my hips and thighs have begun to fill out size 3 low-rise jeans from the junior's department at Macy's. My figure is starting to look, as my mom calls it, womanly.

"Better enjoy it while it lasts," she says to me whenever I eat a whopper-add-bacon (my favorite). I am reminded of the impending doom that is a woman's body. A slow metabolism will soon destroy the freedom to eat whatever food I want, unless I can stomach the consequences.

I like to sit at the kitchen table to flip through the pages of *Us Weekly* when I am in the mood to be inspired by the latest fashion trends or want to research my ongoing reinvention. I beg my mom for a subscription, and she gives in, but only for a limited time because although she too doesn't mind all the celebrity chisme, it is expensive. I pride myself on the tiny facts I know—the names of each of Brangelina's kids and their countries of origin, the number of tracks on Lindsay Lohan's *Speak*, and how many of my lifetimes Demi Moore is Ashton Kutcher's senior (just over one.) I like knowing the answers to questions.

I wear slimy Crest Whitestrips for 30 minutes, twice daily, in the two weeks leading up to my freshman yearbook portrait. I book a picture day appointment at the mall to get my makeup done at MAC and probably just buy a single tube of clear Lipglass or one shimmery plum eyeshadow for the exchange. I also plan a haircut at my cousin's wife salon and ask her for Lindsay Lohan sideswept bangs with beachy curling iron waves. My eyebrows are waxed to a perfect three hair follicles wide. I wear the collar of my Abercrombie and Fitch polo popped and the buttons open to show off the diamond cross necklace my dad gave me. Later in the year, I will alternate my looks by wearing two popped collars in contrasting colors at once.

My mom says I look very pretty, and she seems proud of me for the first time in a long time.

I think I am hot shit and I think I will also be proud of this photo for years to come.

New Emilly is a girl who is destined for Good People Things. She is supposed to get 3.0s or higher, and her freshman year of high school will be perfect. This will be her very own *Princess*

Diaries moment. She will have it all—best friends, a boyfriend, good grades, extra curriculars, and maybe even a better relationship with her dad.

I decide I would like to run for student government. I hear this is the kind of stuff that looks good on college applications. Having the power to plan events and sway school activities is a fun bonus. I run a campaign with a couple other girls and dub our trio the Dream Team. I design posters in Photoshop, and we pool our parents' money to have them printed at Kinko's. We spring for the laminated banner too and hang it above the ultra-popular student store that sells Flamin' Hot Cheetos and Welch's Fruit Snacks. I overlay text on each candidate's digital camera selfies, and we post them all over Myspace. We don't know the Dream Team is the same pet name for the lawyers who got OJ acquitted, but luckily neither do the 14-year-olds around us.

I get a message on Myspace from a sophomore named Kylie: "Why the fuck are you talking shit to my girl Molly?" I have no idea who Molly or Kylie are, but it is certainly possible that I talked shit to a girl named Molly. I apologize but tell her she doesn't need to come at me the way she is. This will squash the drama, but only for a while. A sideways glance or a shoulder check in the hall will make it bubble up again, over and over, in the months to come. Many more Myspace messages will be exchanged. I'll look to my friend Heidi and ask her older sister, a wannabe-hood-white girl who is a senior, to scare the sophomore. This will cool things off again for a minute.

When student government election day rolls around, two of the three of the Dream Team makes it. I am elected freshman class secretary, Jamie gets president, and a random white boy from our middle school gets vice president. I also make it onto the JV soccer team. This is surely a feat at a school that is expected to make it to state championships every year, but I am disappointed I didn't immediately get recruited for varsity like my sister Erika did. I do show up for practices, albeit sometimes high or drunk, and attend every game. I hope I don't keep playing like a benchwarmer.

* * *

A few weeks into my first year of high school, I am running miles all the time. I have slowed my daily habit of marijuana and subsequent munchies but I am always late to first period. I try to rectify my lateness by skipping breakfast, so I have one less thing to do to get out of the door and onto the hilly street to school, which is technically two corners away from our house. After all, I am supposed to be good and losing grade points for tardiness is just stupid.

I am hanging out with a certain group of old friends again for my reinvention. It takes us a few weeks into high school to reconnect, but we are a gaggle of girls whose dads are divorced or deadbeats or who have died far too soon. We are connected, even in the years we drift in and out of friendship. And when our crew is back, we easily return to doing stupid (and sometimes deep) shit together. We all still feel familiar. Our crew is made up of me, Krista, Kelly, Monique, and sometimes Evelyn and Becky. We eat weed brownies for breakfast in the quad and slide down carpeted staircases with cardboard sleds when we are bored and hungover. We pick up pink boxes of Chuck's Donuts and laze around eating cinnamon twists, discussing how fucked up the world is. We prefer to get white girl wasted on Bacardi Grand Melón and Mike's Hard. We are girls who get guys, talk back to teachers, never pay for pot, pretend to be good, carry out covert three-way calls, and learn from each other how to be better liars.

My new old friends like to party, and I find out the new version of me still does too. I think I must be wired to crave the feeling of recklessness. I like the power that comes from doing things I know I can get in trouble for. The freeness I feel when only my friends know where I am, when I ignore my mom's 3AM phone calls, customized to play "Locked up" by Akon when she rings, wondering where I am. I like getting away with things most, but I still don't even care the times I get caught.

I am welcomed into the lengthy beautification ritual that happens before we go out. We swap makeup and clothes, and pre-game so we don't have to share our alcohol with mooches later, and it all feels sacred. I come to realize that as a size 3, fitting into my friends' zero or one jeans is going to be difficult, but I want to die every time they ask to try on a pair of mine. There is something acutely humiliating about watching someone pull up the denim you must wiggle your ass left and right to wedge into, the denim you must suck in and lay back on a bed to button, and when they do the same, the pull-up motion is singular, and unsavory pockets of air appear everywhere making them unwearable. This exchange of pants and my wanting to shrink in response happens over and over, every single weekend. And eventually it happens on weeknights too.

* * *

Nicole Richie and Mary Kate Olsen are my favorite celebrities. They rock edgy boho looks and I call them my style icons even though I won't be bold enough to wear any shades of brown until the end of my sophomore year. At first their frail frames shock me, but MK and Nicole become my inspiration. I like that they seem different from the other average Hollywood stars. Their style and tiny size set them apart.

I don't notice when I go from looking at their bodies with horror to looking at their protruding bones with delight. I begin to wish their bodies were mine. *Delicate* is a word I want for myself too.

At school, I begin getting compliments from the other Abercrombie and Fitch girls for how great I look. I'm getting so fit since I've joined this hyper-competitive soccer team, according to my mom. I hadn't really noticed, but then I do, and I start to enjoy the attention from friends and family and acquaintances. My sense of accomplishment blooms right along the space between my fabric and skin, and every person who notices. This is exceptional. I can be exceptional. I add thinness to my list of having it all.

* * *

Our clique begins to sit at one of two mesh picnic tables by 'A' hall at lunch. The tables overlook the football field and there is a group of sophomore guys from San Carlos that occupy the other mesh table. One by one, the San Carlos guys and my best friends begin to date.

I secretly hate people from San Carlos off the bat, at least a little, because San Carlos is even richer than already-rich Belmont is. I think there is a special type of asshole-ness reserved for kids who come from hella money, and high school only further cements this truth. I learn the San Carlos guys who sit across from us chew to pass the time, and the flesh above their respective jawlines are often bulging. They use Coke cans to dispose of gnawed mounds of Skoal tobacco, soppy with saliva, and one day at a party I'll accidentally take a sip from a beer can they've used in the same way.

I will also eventually learn that these are the type of white boys who get sentenced to community service for DUIs—totaling their BMW is punishment enough—and who only get probation for manslaughter because boys will be boys and because accidentally sucker punching another boy to the back of the head—and to his death—outside of the Giants stadium is an honest mistake.

But this is the beginning of high school, and none of that has happened yet, and so we sit and watch these tall-tee-wearing, Mac

Dre- and E-40-listening, Natty Ice- and Mickey's 40's-drinking white boys with hearts thumping, mouths salivating every time they look our way. Krista is naturally the first to get with someone, and she hooks up with Scott. Then Kelly gets with Trevor. With Monique and me, it's always a competition and, like usual, we have the same taste, which is the sole Latino in their group. He goes to another school, so we only see him when we hang out after school. Mark isn't either of our type and so the only one left is Anthony.

Anthony Garcia says he's from the wrong side of the tracks but he's still from Belmont. When he says this, I know it is technically true in a Belmont sense, but it's not really what they mean in movies or rap songs when they say that kinda thing. I don't bother trying to correct him because at least he is not a rich kid from San Carlos.

Anthony is one lanky motherfucker, looming over six feet tall with a nose hook bigger than mine and skin the same shade as the Hanes shirts he likes to rock past his knees. When me and Anthony hang out alone, he's sweet. He makes me laugh. We have actual conversations, and he says more than just "this song slaps" between shots of vodka or sips of Coors, which is pretty much the extent of what the other dudes say in my direction, if anything at all.

Anthony trusts me enough to buzz an 'A' into his hair with clippers and he shares his weed and we sometimes stop by the Wendy's near the house where he and his mom live to eat (I order kids' meals). He's thoughtful: he brings me a souvenir—a wooden pipe hand-carved with two people fucking on it—back from a family trip to Mexico. He's the one who helps me find my T-Mobile Sidekick at a party when his rich dick friends try to steal it by throwing it onto the roof. But around his boys, Anthony's also quick to call girls "hoes" and point out that the Garcia in his name comes from Spain, not Mexico. He also doesn't stick up for me when Scott and Camden kick my backpack to each other after school one day, over and over, and my glasses end up broken. When a friend calls Camden on speaker phone in front of me to secretly confront him, Camden says he doesn't know why he was kicking on my backpack, but he doesn't care because "I'm hella ugly." I jot this down in my diary. *Hella ugly.* I write that I'm upset he said it but more upset at myself for being bothered by *something I've heard so many times before.* A handful of pages and weeks later, I will write that Camden is one of the sweetest guys at school.

One day when we are hanging together alone after school, Anthony tells me he likes me so much.

He says I am "hella cool."

He tells me he wishes he could be my boyfriend—but.

When I ask, "But what," he says something like, "But I can't date you because my friends would make fun of me."

I can't find words. I think there is a good chance I'm not going to like his response, but I don't know what else to say and I fill the silence by asking why once more.

My throat is small. Maybe his throat will be too small to answer.

But after only a tiny pause, Anthony says he can't date me because I'm Mexican. Even though *he* doesn't care, his friends would never stop making fun of him.

I don't expect this answer.

I think all I say back is, "Oh."

* * *

I am halfway through my freshman year. It is the beginning of a new semester and year, and I think 2006 is sure to be special. I've just gotten braces and my mom is thankfully cool with spending the extra bit of money on a clear top row so they're not as obvious as the metal ones I wear on my bottom row. My grades have begun to slip a bit, but I think I still have time to catch up.

One afternoon, I'll have chosen to get into my first fist-fight mere feet from where my Dream Team banner hung at the precise stroke of the lunch bell. The quad will be our ring and students will hang from the fence nearby to get a better glimpse. I'll admit to my premeditation in the principal's office with a smile and lay out the case: months of *escalating* Myspace messages—The Sophomore Kylie Cyberbullying The Freshman Emilly—printed in full color, a saved voicemail on my Sidekick from Kylie telling me to meet her at a gas station [to get jumped], and I'll point to the safety I desired of a public fight on campus easily broken up by security—the extra rings I armed myself with a secret, already tucked back into my pants pocket. I'll lose my title of freshman class secretary and earn the second suspension of my academic career, but I'll have at least won back my cred of being a tough bitch not to be fucked with. A freshman beating up a sophomore, a coconut freshman yanking the white girl sophomore's puka shell necklace apart and watching it sprinkle the cement, and a freshman who tried to spit on the sophomore after winning the fight, glowing from glory. A freshman who handled matters on her own instead of being a rat tattling to the principal. I squash the beef on my own and end the drama for good.

On another less momentous day at lunch, Monique introduces me to her pretty-eyed boyfriend, Alan, who is from East Palo Alto. Alan and his crew hang over by the chain link fence on the way to the theater building (which I have never and will never step foot in), and this is where I first meet Cristian Wexler. Cristian, who goes by his last name, is also a junior, like Alan, and from EPA. He has 'Wexler' tattooed on his right bicep in Edwardian Script. He wears his curls big and uses an afro Afro pick even though his hair isn't more than 3a. He is nicaragüense,

Guatemalan, Mexican, and his also-out-of-the-picture dad is German, he explains, hence the Wexler.

At first, I'm not so sure about Wexler. But then we start texting every day. Texting becomes long phone calls becomes falling asleep together on our cellies. Next comes ditching the picnic benches for the fence at lunch.

Wexler begins walking me to all my classes. I wear his boxy black peacoat when I am cold. I live for the anticipation between periods and that moment after the bell rings when we find each other in the halls, lock eyes, link fingers, smile wide, and just say "hey."

Being around Wexler is intoxicating. My cheeks regularly hurt from cheesing and trying to hide it, so I don't come off as desperate. I finally understand what people mean when they say they have butterflies in their bellies. I think I am in love. I write in my diary that I worry I am more into him than he is into me. *At least I know what infatuation feels like*, I write, and it feels so good.

A few weeks into courting, it's Valentine's Day. I've decided to skip the cliché of a box of chocolates and flowers that'll wilt for something that will last him forever: I head to Hillsdale Mall where I adopt a white, pink-nosed Build-a-Bear. I dress him in scarlet silk heart boxers with red and blush bows for each ear and accessorize him with a plush box of chocolates. He, Wexler Jr., comes in a special crimson cardboard Valentine's Day house. I also stop by a kiosk that's like the Things Remembered store but cooler because I get to pick out a dog tag necklace, provide the attendant with a photo of Wexler's friend who passed, and they engrave it with her picture and "RIP." It feels nice to rub the tag between my thumbs—the bumpy right next to the smooth. I hope Wexler thinks to get me something nice too.

When February 14th rolls around, I am ushered, eyes covered by Monique's hands, to my surprise. Though I've never really liked when friends touch me like this or hug me too long, I suck it up for the reveal in between classes. I don't care for the sensation of Monique's clammy hands or unwanted breath on my neck, but when I open my eyes, I find it has been worth it. I am bestowed with a full-blown hallway spectacle of one dozen red roses, a Safeway balloon bouquet, and a goofy-hat-wearing lime green stuffed prince charming frog. It is the ultimate tribute maybe always but especially for a freshman in high school. At 11:59PM that night, Wexler asks me to be his girl before we fall asleep together on the phone.

My boyfriend and I begin to let lunchtime last beyond its allotted window. We ditch class to make out (and more) in the near-abandoned T-wing hallways. I've been skipping out eating lunch to maximize my time spent hanging out with Wexler ever since we met, and now, even when we walk to different corners of campus and he sometimes stops by the southernmost student store where the Tongans and Samoans hang out, I say I'm not hungry. The truth is I don't want to end up with chips stuck in my braces and I am getting used to the constant feeling of hunger. I am learning to ignore it. I tell myself I am in full-on love, which is, in some ways, true. I am consumed by what it feels like to be in the intimate presence of another human, of being embraced by wide-reaching arms, of feeling small when I rest my head against his chest, of thinking how out of literally one thousand other girls at school, I'm the one he picked.

My grades slip worse, until I'm dubbed a delinquent. It's easy to scrub the voicemail clean of automated messages before my mom gets home from work. Every time I press the delete button, I grin, thinking how school administrators are so stupid to give us a name they think shames us, but it ultimately just makes me feel more like a badass. I have never liked being told what I can or can't do, and I never will. It makes me giddy how effortlessly I can make their narc asses disappear.

A few more weeks into deep lust, I write in my diary that I've been *noticing shit* about Wexler lately. He deletes all the sweet comments I leave on his Myspace page. He has other girls in his top 8, but not me. I've developed and scanned the pics we took on my disposable camera and uploaded them to Photobucket. My favorites are a tie between the one where Wexler is in his wife beater, tongue and tatt out, and I'm looking over with a subtle smile, or the one we took above the quad stairs and I'm wearing his jacket and you can tell, for once, I know and feel how beautiful I look.

But Wexler has none of these loving pics on his page—only ones with other girls. Worse maybe is that at school, when we hold hands, he's begun to stuff both our hands into his pockets like he's trying to hide them.

I don't think he's bein' real with me, I write. *I want him to be though. I want him to care about me as much as I care about him. I want him to want me as much as I want him. I want him to wanna be with me as much as I wanna be with him, and it's killing me because I know I don't have control over the situation. He says I'm trippin' whenever I bring it up.*

I write again that I'm afraid I am more into him than he is into me. What I don't write is that I think Wexler is ashamed of me, and I don't know why he doesn't want me anymore. I see now, clear as Visine eyes, I was being played. But I couldn't see it then.

I am broken up with over the Internet and after many slow weeks of a glacial ghosting on his end. We continue to argue on AIM for far too long after we break up. I am heartbroken and pissed.

For years, I will tell myself that Camila started calling me a slut and threatening to fight me because she was a jealous puta with too much allegiance for her friend Cristian. But in my diary, I write Wexler instant messaged me that he was going to get someone to *beat my ass since he couldn't do it himself.* I write that I'm confused and scared and that he's on some psycho boy shit. I don't tell anyone, and I would've kept believing Camila was the only monster were it not for my diary all these years later. Even now, my mind's fucked-up instinct is to wonder what awful things I must've said to provoke him.

After our relationship ends, I think I am almost as sad as I was when I didn't want to live through middle school. I'll find out Wexler was hooking up with Lili, another Latina girl, behind my back. I try to start eating again in the mornings, or at least eat lunch, but I find that I never feel hungry enough to want to eat. I tell myself I will only skip lunch when I forget my cash. I pretend not to realize I can borrow money from friends. I tell myself I'm just forgetful when I stop asking my mom for lunch money altogether.

* * *

There are suddenly stretches of time I must occupy on my own after school. My friends are still my crew, but everyone has boyfriends and are sometimes busy. When I am home alone, all I have is myself and the deep, familiar pit of loneliness and unlovability. I pass the hours by not doing homework and instead endlessly scroll and click and lurk on Myspace. I do this over and over until all that is bright is my face lit from the computer screen, and my mom comes home and asks why I am sitting in the dark.

Eventually I find a secret group of people on the Internet who welcome me in with proudly frail arms. They are goal-oriented girls seeking gaunt cheeks and chiseled clavicle bones. They gush over each other's successes without shame and readily share helpful tips for controlling their form. They post *thinspiration*— pictures of Amy Winehouse, Victoria Beckham, and all of my favorite idols. They worship ballerina bodies—elegantly curved birds with small bones dotting down their spines. They—we—are the ProAna community, and they are teaching me new definitions for motivation. I join them in pledges to no longer drink anything besides water or alcohol, empty calories, and they applaud me. I learn how to count caloric intake and how to punish myself when I don't follow our rules. They cheer me on. I post a picture of my concave belly, hip bones bruised from a night in the front row of an Expendables concert in Santa Cruz. They say I look so fragile. I like to be praised. I like to feel important in my own private community, and I feel as though I've finally found a way to earn beauty. All I have to do is work harder.

I think my body has become accustomed to only asking, or listening, for food once per day. I decide rather than listen to my body and wait for the hunger to come, my body will learn to listen to me. I will choose to keep waiting. My lifestyle is now a choice I can make.

My GPA plummets into the 1.0s. An Abercrombie and Fitch girl who used to ask me what my GPA was in middle school now asks me how much I weigh instead. Numbers remain our competition, and I am proud to report my new weight class. She asks how I keep my weight down in the "one-ohs." I don't tell her any of my secrets.

08. (when ya gonna) give it up to me

Did you know one in three Latinas will become pregnant before the age of 20? I sure as hell do, thanks to the enthusiastic white lady from Planned Parenthood who seared it into my brain during one of her visits to our biology class near the end of ninth grade.

Mr. Schnitz, with his knobby knees, bow ties, and four eyes, could instruct chromosomal curriculum and meiosis in his sleep, yet any steps beyond XY and XX would have caused him a malfunction. He was real sweet and probably loved listening to Coldplay on CD with his wife, but Mr. Schnitz stepped back to let the nice white lady do the talking when it came to the XXX.

Barb was a safe sex zealot. She had dark hair and wasn't super old yet—30 tops—and giggled as she released new facts into the classroom, letting them linger a little too long before saying another. She seemed equal parts excited and nervous, like the first day I worked at Toys 'R' Us after getting away with lying about my birthday so I could work more hours. But Barb went above and beyond: there were anatomically correct plastic genitalia in different colors and sizes, pop quizzes—multi-choice and fill-in-the-blank, and maybe even a condom-covered banana. Between facts, she'd offer her wisdom. The small, latched red plastic Caboodle she brought to class had a slit in the top and students could insert their folded up, top-secret sex questions. She'd answer them aloud. About one in two were jokes.

I can't recall how my own pregnancy odds stacked up against the other *minorities* and underserved youth in the classroom, but I do remember it was so bad, she repeated it twice. "Ooonnne in threeeee," she hissed, gaze oscillating, slowly turning her gaze around the beige linoleum box of a classroom to everyone, but especially wide-eyed at the handful of Black and brown girls in the room. The second time she said it I think it echoed out into the hallway, what with all the doom and gloom she shoved out alongside it.

I'm sure the nice white lady didn't mean to single me, or us statistically *at-risk* girls, out in that suburban Bay Area high school classroom designed by a guy who designed the state's prisons. But when you're the hairy shell of a coconut in a sea of tender and sweet white meat, it's impossible not to feel like you've already fucked up a little bit. Plus, I knew if I was immediately tallying up my classmates and doing the math to predict which one of us would get pregnant on account of science, smug ass Timmy from the San Carlos hills sure was too.

All my life, I've been dodging the shitty statistics of being a Brown Girl in America. *Most Likely to Be a Dropout. Most Likely to Attempt Suicide. Most Likely to Do Drugs. Most Likely to Become a Teen Mom™.*

I had already achieved two superlatives on the list, and a real one for Best Hair in middle school, but being a teen mom scared me the most. So, all I had to do was make it six more years to avoid falling victim to another Brown Girl Stat.

"Did you know if you get pregnant, you only have one of three options?" The nice instructor lady taught us that one, too.

You can keep it, give it away, or have an abortion. There was a one in three chance I'd have to make that decision. I could keep it and become a mom that almost flunked out of eighth grade but then dropped out to raise her baby as best as she could by working at Toys 'R' Us for 20 years. I could look up an adoption How-To online to figure out how to give my baby away to a family, but they would have to be cool and rich and not racist, which would be hard to find. I could also take a $500 pill and make it go away if I had enough time, or suck it out with a $500 vacuum if I had less time.

Between me, and my cousin Amanda, and my cousin Isela—one of us was destined, statistically speaking, to make the mistake of getting knocked up before really reaching adulthood. Amanda was really good at soccer, Isela was really rich, and I was the one really trying—but failing—with a 1.4 GPA freshman year.

Right in the thick of figuring out whether we should take French or Spanish as an elective, sneak in peppermint schnapps or sour apple gin to the bowling alley, find a dress to wear to the homecoming dance, or pick out where we might apply to college one day, one in three of us would suddenly be forced to squeeze in some time to decide one of three choices for what to do with the growing embryo embedded in our body. *Fuck that.*

* * *

In truly modern, holier-than-thou Catholic girl fashion, I told my boyfriends and best friends I was going to wait a full calendar year (not school year) before it was my turn to have sex for the first time. It was the decent thing to do, and it would buy me some time.

When I "dated" Danny in middle school and a little bit into high school, he was a high school junior who lived in South City. Our relationship subsisted of late-night AIM chats, hours-long calls on our Nokia cell phones, and lofty-ass letters sent via snail mail because I'd watched *The Notebook* a few too many times. We made out exactly once. It was in the parking lot of a Daly City mall. We had spent the day holding hands through the food court and I had watched him unfurl his fingers all up on that PlayStation controller in the back of the Zumiez skate shop. He was Filipino and Black, and my cousin's friends' cousin. We dated for three months maybe, but, according to my diary, really nine months (long enough to incubate a baby) if you included the "talking" stage. I think Danny might be the first boyfriend who cheated on me.

At home, The Talk was limited to my single mama telling me to "Be saaaaaafe," in a sing-songy, hella sarcastic tone. She'd top off the plea with a cringy half smile, her lips painfully pursed, and a few wiggles from her raised eyebrows.

"Guys don't like girls who are easy," she would warn.

After my relationship with Wexler ended, and we maxed out at third base on school property, I wonder if she's right. The action was equal parts gross and exciting, but afterwards, he was the one who got a girl in his grade to shove me and call me a "hoe" in the hall even though he was the *man hoe* who had been cheating on me.

* * *

At the very end of that freshman year, I met Damien. He was a senior and an 18-year-old virgin. I was still a freshman. *The Omen* had just been re-released.

Damien's hair was black, he lived out in the part of the hood— EPA—that was beginning to be gentrified, and he unironically still wore a chain on his trifold fabric wallet. He was the first guy I ever wore a couple's costume with. He was my first long-term relationship. When I was a sophomore in high school and he was at community college, I wore a midriff referee costume and he wore a basketball jersey for our first Halloween together.

The Playboy bunny jewelry I swapped in after getting my belly button pierced at Rubin's in The Mission (the same sketchy place I'll later go to get my lip ring) dangled out in the open and drew eyes down towards my protruding hip bones. This would be the first time Abercrombie and Fitch girls would ask me if my skinny was dangerous—if I was an anorexic. This would be the first of many times I would shrug and laugh them off.

On our first year together celebrating Damien's birthday, I bought him knock-off Girbauds with royal blue straps off eBay. I used the account I made a few months earlier to sell desperate families the new Tickle Me Elmo at a significant markup beyond the ten-percent retail discount I earned as a Toys 'R' Us employee. For my birthday, Damien gave me a framed picture of a rose he'd had since he won it at a carnival when he was 13 years old. He said he always knew he'd give it to the woman he'd be with for the rest of his life.

With a boyfriend in the picture, my time thinned, as did I. I slowly started swapping out best friend dates for boyfriend dates. For a while, I tried fusing the two groups like a desperate stepmom trying to blend her new family, but it didn't work. He told me my best friends Krista and Kelly were too immature.

He had tried to woo me one night into a childhood bedroom deflowering when my mom was still home, which was gross because:

A. I couldn't even think of doing it in the same house as my mom.

B. We never talked about having sex before he tried to put the moves on me.

Eventually, we talked it out. I guess I hadn't really known what I was proving by waiting exactly 12 months. And if I was going to be with this guy forever, like we both said, what was a few months sooner in the long run?

I lost my V-Card seven months in. It happened at a party in a giant beachside house an 18-year-old senior rented out for the weekend. The house was too big on its own, but it was even more oversized considering there were only about a dozen kids there. We drank flavored vodka from plastic red cups and the white boys in tall tees clutched their Mickey's. Beer pong happened on the deck overlooking the black ocean. It wasn't even prom.

I remember thinking the queen linen set in the master bedroom Damien had called dibs on, with its matching embroidered bed skirt and stiff brown pillowcases, was very adult. As we laid in some random adults' bedroom, I heard giggling. Krista and Kelly were crawling on the carpeted floor trying to sneak it. I would have thought it was funny, except it was My First Time. They repeated the shenanigan twice over. The intermittent intrusions, shouting of "Chug! Chug! Chug" outside the door, and beige sheets were *not* like *The Notebook*. We used a condom.

* * *

Over the next year or so I drifted further away from my friends and dove into playing grown up with my older boyfriend. We spent nights together regularly. He looked through my phone regularly. We'd fight, and I'd be the one apologizing regularly. We had sex less and less regularly.

I repeated the mistakes of my own absent father and started making out with a 22-year-old Toys 'R' Us coworker, adding Rafael's name into my phone as Rachel. Damien was amazed at how quickly I'd become close with my new friend. I was amazed at how easy it was to be like my father.

After journaling in the blue-and-pastel diary my sister, Erika, gifted me since middle school, Damien found it. He confronted me about some things I had written. I had seen Julian, a Redwood City guy at a barbecue I once thought I might date, earlier that day. I had given Julian my number and wrote that when a 650 number came in later that night, I had wanted to answer. I figured it could be Julian, but it was 11 PM and Damien was coming over soon and I knew I wouldn't have a good enough lie for either guy when the time would come to get off the phone. I joked about having written about Julian once before in my diary and signing off as *The Future Mrs. Julian Torralba.*

When Damien confronted me about it, for a moment, I felt bad. I imagined him reading through the diary of the teenager he thought was the love of his life. Perhaps, he was seeking danger, but I knew he was seeking reaffirmation, confirmation, validation, reciprocation of his love for me. He sought the same *Notebook* love letters dripping in poetic flourish. He sought recapitulations of our dates to The Cheesecake Factory, of lacing fingers while drinking vodka mixed with Powerade on the way to Giants games. He sought dreams of a future that included him.

"I love you," I'd repeat to Damien, even after I was no longer sure I meant it. I had learned to keep my eye contact steady, never quivering or wandering even half a millisecond. I had read that cops could pick out liars from a line up, on account of whether or not their eyes darted when their names were called, if they stuttered when they spoke, or if their voices ended on a high note like their bodies couldn't help but claw, reach, call up to God for forgiveness.

I had trained myself to come off like a truth teller. But housed in the pages of that hardcover diary, the truth ran free. My truth felt safe and protected from the judgement that existed on the outside.

What Damien found in these pages was not gratitude nor awe nor speak of any fate drawing the pair together. What Damien found in these pages were the words of an unhappy girl. A girl with untreated clinical depression. A girl who had crushes on boys who weren't Damien. A girl who felt stuck.

So, Damien did what real men, real machistas do after reading girls' diaries. He curled his fingers into a ball, pumping and pulsing to push out any semblance of air between his flesh. His eyes locked with mine and the brown of his irises were gone. His pupils, charcoal black, swelled wildly before they narrowed to match mine. Our eyes fell, and then he wiped at his black eyes with a free hand. A tear? He cocked his elbow back and almost paused before sending his fist into the bumpy butter yellow drywall of my childhood bedroom. The *Juno* poster hanging above my bed clung onto dear life by a corner of its frame. The indentation of his knuckles was neatly impressed. It is still there.

I stopped writing in my diary.

Three months later, I broke up with him for the first time. The journal should have been the last straw, but it was not. This break-up only lasted two months. We got back together and had more regular missionary sex. We used more condoms. Then we broke up again my junior year. Three weeks after that break-up, I realized I had missed my period. I was 17 years old. I had never missed a period in my seven years of having one.

* * *

Tia Sylvia was 20 when she had Martin. Abuelita was 20 when she had my mom. My mom was 19 when she had Erika.

Maybe it was just my turn to be one in three.

I went to school and pretended everything was normal for the next few days. I tried not to think about the looming possibility of a swift end to my youth. Instead, I thought about the classmates who'd gotten pregnant over the years, right before my eyes.

When I was in the seventh grade, an eighth grader got pregnant by her eighth-grade boyfriend. When they had the baby, her parents made her pretend it was her younger brother. In high school, she and her boyfriend were still together and were still slipping up. She got pregnant again and had to transfer to Redwood—the alternative school for students who disrupt classrooms with outbursts of rage and/or swelling bellies. That's where Wexler's best friend was sent, too, after she got pregnant junior year. It's also where Wexler went after he set a piece of plastic to spin in the science lab microwave for eight minutes and it caught fire.

Rumors swirled that admin shipped pregnant girls off to Redwood so the good girls wouldn't be tempted to get pregnant too, but I knew teen pregnancies weren't all bad. I'd seen failing schoolmates turn their shit around and graduate for the sake of their babies. I'd seen pregnant girls get permission to prioritize themselves for the first time in their lives. I'd seen pregnant girls become women and remain kick ass mothers while growing up alongside their babies the whole way. Teen mamas had raised my own sister and cousins and friends, and I would be a kick ass mama if it became my destiny too.

* * *

On the drive home from school later that week, I decided I couldn't wait any longer to uncover my fate. The pregnancy test commercials had confused me into thinking I had to wait five days or two weeks or something before taking the test. I tried to do the math but didn't know where to start.

I thought about stopping into the local Planned Parenthood I frequented to stuff my backpack with handfuls of novelty flavored condoms, but I didn't want to run into anyone I knew. The last thing I needed was to have it become known that I was maybe possibly carrying my ex-boyfriend's baby. He definitely couldn't know, and neither could anyone else.

I parked my second-hand Toyota 4Runner in the driveway of my house instead. I don't remember if it was cold or not, but I put on a black hoodie just for the occasion and stretched the hood over my head as far as it would go. I walked down the steep hill with my head down towards the shopping center.

As a kid, I always complained about the walk because I knew the way back wouldn't be so easy. Sometimes my mom made us walk and sometimes we drove down, but we'd get ice cream together in the evenings. I'd normally get chocolate chip cookie dough but on occasion would request Daquiri Ice because I thought it was scandalous and impressive and adult. My mom ordered Jamoca Almond Fudge every time. My little brother, Hector, would get Rainbow Sherbet and coat his entire face with sticky, peach-colored froth. Erika was the embodiment of her pick: Rocky Road. Baskin-Robbins was the first job I applied to and was rejected from.

On this day, I skipped the ice cream shop and headed straight into the second job I applied to. Luigi's Market seemed to only hire eerily similar bougie white boys who belonged in the neighborhood to stock their shelves with overpriced jars of opulence. Luigi's was my second rejection.

I picked the furthest entrance to the store and weaved past the still-warm baguettes, chocolate sprinkle cupcakes, and wheels of parmesan cheese. In the aisle north of the canned artichoke hearts and sundried tomatoes, I found the medicine. I had a problem that needed fixing, but pregnancy tests weren't a medicine, it turns out. I moved to the next aisle and there— between the single bottle of K-Y Jelly lube and fancy floral adult diapers—were a row of pregnancy tests. I crouched down and picked the cheapest one.

I held it at my hip, close to my body, and moved towards the checkout stands. I had two options: The open register with a boy from school standing behind it and another boy from school ready to bag or register number two where a woman's groceries were being bagged in plastic by an older gentleman.

The boys laughed and waved their arms to get my attention. The older man told me the other register was open. I pretended I was invisible and didn't hear a thing. They all shrugged.

When it was my turn, I placed my test, face-down, on the conveyor belt and momentarily stared the store clerk in the eye. We said nothing, and I handed him a single crumpled-up $20 bill from my pocket. He placed the test, and my change, in a small brown paper bag which I stuffed into my hoodie's kangaroo pouch.

At home I sat on the toilet, peeing on the white plastic stick. The opening scene of *Juno* ran through my mind. At least I wasn't doing this in public, but maybe I should have drunk Sunny D?

My eyes welled up as I laid on the cramped bathroom floor waiting—the stick of pee-covered plastic dangling on the edge of the sink. I noticed the bathmat smelled like dog pee again. A lightbulb above the wood vanity mirror flickered. There was a hole in the wall from where my brother once pulled the towel rack down too hard. I thought about my ex-boyfriend Damien— the one who might be the father of my unborn child—and the fucking hole he tried to punch in my bedroom wall. I covered up the dent from his bloody knuckles with my *Juno* poster.

The alarm on my phone went off.

I held my breath. I sat up. I grabbed the test and tried to steady it, then looked: a single blue line.

I cried.

A brilliant case of inverse math; a negative, but truly a positive. I stopped holding my breath.

I thought about how happy I was that my child wasn't here yet. How happy I was that I didn't have to make the choice of whether I wanted to take options one, two, or three. I thought about how lucky I was to still have some of my own childhood left.

He is not the father, I thought a la *Maury*, not quite ready to muster up a laugh. My hand was still shaking. I was still spooked.

I picked the plastic bag out of the garbage bin and pushed the pregnancy test to the bottom, straight through the crumbled-up tissues and yellowed Q-tips. I couldn't take any chances. I put my hoodie back up and walked it outside to the curbside trash.

The next day, I bled through my underwear. I nearly cried again. *Three more years.*

09. por qué me haces llorar

My Papi's family is old school. The adults stand in clusters at parties and when we younger familia arrive, we must walk from huddled group to group and interrupt them with greetings. The señoras get a small handshake or hug and a fake kiss—our cheeks touch, turned, and we pucker at the air in unison. The señores get a handshake, and sometimes a fake kiss too if you know how they're related to you. Parties happen several times a year—Easter, bautizos, first communions, birthdays, deaths. The parties are big—no fewer than fifty guests in attendance with linen-covered table rentals, buffet or taquero, mariachi and/or a DJ, and plenty of tequila, vino, y cerveza. How many people successfully pull off the "Payaso de Rodeo" line dance determines exactly how cool a party is.

If it takes us 22 minutes to enter a party, it takes at least two times longer to leave when we make the rounds again because more adults have inevitably arrived, and the alcohol makes way for the truer, blunter, lengthier things they want to get off their minds like why we don't come around more often or if we know our Papi loves us? My sister and I have learned that if we don't follow the rules, somebody will tell somebody and then somebody else will tell our dad, even if he isn't there, and everyone will know we are disrespectful. Growing up, I often felt that our mere presence as bastard children—as the first family—was a disrespect, or at least another reason to be more scrutinized. It was like we were seen as washed-up child stars doomed for misery and, worse, poverty.

My Papi believes elders deserve our undying respect. He believes there are rules for how we must behave, and I have been taught to follow these.

"No andas con esas caras," he'd say to me when, so often, my face would betray my attempts at obedience. "Your face is going to get stuck like that," my mom would sometimes chime in.

Even though my Papi is the one who was born in Redwood City and my Mami was born in Apatzingán, he is the more Mexican one having been raised there. My Mami would agree. Other rules I have learned: don't talk back, asking questions is talking back, don't cry—that's talking back, say please and thank you, repeat these—with a smile—if someone else decides you sound insincere, dress for parties with a full-body commitment; you will be judged by the smoothness of your hair to the colored polish of your toenails to the slimness of your waistline and everything in between, men are heads of the house and can do as they please, our women aren't afraid to physically fight even at family parties, and only cry when you can blame the tequila (or corridos).

* * *

There is a years-long stretch of time when my mother and father speak every week. My Mami, mid-dishwashing, would rinse herself of suds, turn off the kitchen sink, then wipe her hands with a towel as quickly as she could to make sure she'd pick up our home phone by the second or third ring. Neck cranked to one side, cradling the receiver, she'd finish drying her hands with her jeans and would make the short walk down the hall to the bedroom they once shared. She'd lay on her back over the made bed, pick up the beige ringlet-corded phone from the nightstand, and hang up the wireless one. Then they'd talk. Sometimes she'd twirl her soft hair or the curled cord or pick out lint from her belly button. They'd do this for a long time.

She says they'd talk about us, her kids. She'd tell him about what we were up to, what we needed, and probably how much money he should send. I can't imagine there'd be hours of conversation to be had about their three babies, but somehow there was. I don't remember if they'd say they loved each other at the end, or silently in their heads, but I think this could be a possibility. I wonder if my Mami was like a therapist, taking in all the ways he was trying to work through his being fucked up, or perhaps helping him see the ways he still was, or the ways he'd grown, or if this was just another space for my Mami to keep up the hope that he could be changed, or really want change. My Mami believes people can change. My Mami believes, and feels it in her own bones, how life is not just. How good people can get hurt just as easily as the bad. How the ones who puff up their chests to pretend they are all edges are usually the most sad and soft. No one is innocent in her eyes and everyone hurts and has been hurt in their own ways. She holds so much love for others, but not very often for herself in the same way. I think I have learned these same lessons from her.

"My parents actually have a great relationship," I'd tell the nosy parents of friends or teammates who'd inquire about the structure of my fragmented family.

"Wow, you are lucky," they'd all say.

And then, "My parents have a great relationship," was only true for half a decade. As the sad-ass saying goes, I suppose all good things must come to end.

My sister's riff with our stepmother, when Erika was 17 or 18, was the tidal wave that damaged everything around it. My Mami and Papi's cordial relationship was swallowed, and my 10-year-old Emilly song lyric comparisons were respawned. I still don't know the details of their riff in full, but I know I am tired of picking at scabs. I think all parties involved would tell a different side of their story. I think all versions could be summarized with broken trust and stupidity and a silver ring maybe-stolen by my sister and our cousin from Camy and a maybe-joke gone wrong and most of all: nobody on any side wanting to back down. I still think about sides now—how we have each other's back until we don't, and how blood always comes first, but how sometimes there are exceptions when your blood flows through so many veins. I think everyone is guilty. I think we all need therapy. I know I am tired of asking what went wrong.

* * *

Mami and Papi go most of four years without talking. Child support requests are delivered via texts or voicemail. I am 17, having made it through high school. I even graduate from the alternative program I enrolled in early. My sister goes on to community college and then moves to San Francisco with her boyfriend. She is punished by having tuition support from my dad withheld for moving in with her boyfriend-now-husband before marriage and winds up with a mountain of student debt. Hector does middle school. We've been raising a puppy named GT—a tribute to my sister's sapphire Mustang Gran Turismo. My Mami and Papi only see each other at our graduations. Our fragments have started to form islands.

My mother's belly is round again, for the fourth time. It is 2008. She is 40 years old. It has been 13 years since the last time. She tells people this baby is a miracle.

My Mami has finally found lasting love in a dog park by our house. She says she's learned to *get over* her new love's thick Peruvian accent. I think his telenovela looks help—slicked black hair, sharp jaw, stick-straight posture, and chiseled arms. She asks the doctors to untie her tubes so she can gift her childless partner one of his own. People, including her children for many years to come, don't need to know this baby was created with the miracle of science. An expensive and oh-so-worthy petri dish. I think the procedures she'd get maybe lined up with the time she said she was going in for gallbladder surgery. I tell this lie to a doctor who asks about my family's medical history. Later, when I learn the truth of her IVF, I am offended by her withholding. I don't understand her reasons, or most reasons, for lying. I wouldn't judge her choices, but I have been lying by proxy. But these secrets are my Mami's own. Secrets are her protection.

* * *

I am still learning to become a better detective. I can't keep track of all the lies of my family, sometimes even my own. I learn more about my dad through whispers in hiding than from my dad himself. Our foundational truths are always cracking. When yet another truth is revealed, my brain has to arrange and rearrange the stories anew. I think my memories look like freeze frames superimposed on translucent cards—sometimes a simple shuffling of the files, of chronology, is in order, other times I think my brain tries to patch newly-burned holes, or maybe my brain decides sometimes the easiest path forward is to shatter ones altogether. I reread my diary entries and see my obsession with truth is one of few constants. I wonder how long my ability to detect lies has been lacking. I wonder if I will ever relearn how to listen to my gut.

"Mi Flacita y mi Erika, look how much you've grown," Papi says to me and my sister one day sitting outside our townhouse.

He has turned off the engine of his pewter Porsche, having returned from a family party. We are perched atop the hill where my Mami raised her three kids in the home where Papi left us.

"Mami, I am so proud of you and your sister," he says.

"You are both becoming such powerful womens."

I suspend a laugh. I am always uneasy with sincerity and direct eye contact, but I feel like a fucking monster for wanting to laugh at my immigrant-ish father for his imperfect English. I think this might be the nicest, realist thing he has ever said to me.

I thank him and let my eyes slowly well. Hearing nice things from adults always makes me uncomfortable—makes the tears want to drop and my throat want to close.

"Don't you think it's not fair that this baby would get part of the house I bought to leave to you and your sister and brother?"

I look Papi in his eyes. I look at our house. I look at the glossy faux-wood interior of this Porsche. His eyes are black and cold, and I am struck by the way they permeate despair after oozing what felt like the warmth of a Michoacán sun. The man who taught me how to avoid eye contact and whose eyes I feared when I gave him the wrong answer or cried because I could not find the words I wanted to use—he has suddenly become a boy. I feel the routine knots in my throat build, fighting from being swallowed. The tiny chills sprinting across my body. The tears priming to push their way out. Already-depleted lungs starved of air, keeping me from breathing.

"No," I say back, keeping the waves of my warble at bay. "That baby is my brother, and that will be his home too."

I can't keep track of all of the lies, but I know I am on the other side of one now. I think about my Mami and how this must be a version of how she felt all those times my Papi asked her to believe him. I am 17.

My father's eyes grow wider. They dare me to stay quiet. I do.

My father's voice growls. This tone, I am more familiar with. He shouts and tries to convince me and my sister of the greed of this fetus. He thinks his loudness and listing all the *nice things* he has done for me and my sister and brother will convince us, but for the first time I know I am the one with the power.

* * *

When I recount this moment to my sister and Mami as an adult, my memories become morphed yet again. My recollection tells me I was all alone, but my sister tells me she was there. My memory of the dialogue—of "womens"—corroborates her presence. I'm not sure why my brain was trying to write her out. My sister thinks we were in a different car: *how would we three have been sitting in a two-seater?* This is a good point too. My brain is still trying to figure out how to rewrite a whole new being into this story. I tell her I swear I remember it was that car, except a growing part of me begins to cast doubt. I think every memory I have and ever have will be shrouded in this same doubt. I tell her I remember that flashy car so vividly, but I don't admit that I hated the flash and maybe that's why it's written itself in. I hated how every time he came to California in a new car, in his name brand attire, every time I witnessed how he and his side of the family wore their wealth, it felt like another reminder of our abandonment, of all the things I wanted but didn't get to have. When I visited my Papi, Camy, and sisters in Chicago, I saw the expanse of their home and land—the John Deer mower Papi had to sit on with a beer because pushing a mower by hand would be far too much for a single human. Another display of the ways his new family were the ones who got it all—the money, the name brands, the father. I tried to drown out the jealousy I felt of my father's love and their things. I tried to live up to his beckoning of undying gratitude and respect.

Years later, when I write this book, my Mami will tell me how she outsmarted my dad with our house. How this young rocky couple used my Mami's name and two cousins to qualify for the mortgage on our house because his income was best left untraceable. How the pair of cousins each came to my Mami in the first decade of ownership requesting to be removed from the title so they could buy houses of their own, and how the last cousin did so six months before the phone call came informing my Mom my Papi would be leaving. How my Mami had earned enough by 30 to refinance on her own in secret—her job security a version of insurance. How in 2008, my Papi tried, for the first time in their relationship, to lawyer up because my Mami was pregnant with the baby of *another man*. How the paper trail evidence that my Papi ever lived in this house did not exist. How my Mami's secret, and her daughters' conviction of what is ours, became the story of our own blood line's protection.

10. you will always bring me flowers

I DIDN'T SEE it coming when I hit rock bottom. Sure, I felt like my life was crumbling—like everything around me was falling apart. Like everything I thought I knew about my life and myself had changed. Like I had lost any semblance of control. Like I, myself, had unraveled.

But I thought all I had to do was be brave, be strong, and remind myself *there are so many other people who have it worse.*

* * *

When I envisioned my 21st birthday, I didn't foresee a wholesome barbeque in the park. I didn't imagine I'd be sipping bottled Coca-Cola through cutesy paper straws I found on Pinterest. I didn't imagine I'd be wearing a nautical navy pin-up dress while I blew out candles with my three-year-old brother on my lap. That my Uncle Baby would be grillin' carne asada; my Abuelita handing out slices of Mexican flag-colored Jell-O. My guests eating chocolate-covered rounds of popcorn after they'd peeled away the plastic wrap and sticker of my face.

I never imagined a 21st birthday in Las Vegas or Cancun either, but I thought the festivities would at least include more friends. Maybe I'd rock a leather fringe skirt, or some ripped up high-waisted pants? Take shotskis and get free drinks simply for being born. I thought there would, no doubt, be a whole fuck-ton more booze.

I didn't think my *ex*-boyfriend's mom would be there, having home-baked a lovely strawberry-and-whipped cream cake, while I couldn't even think of speaking to her son without crying. I never imagined that I'd have to remind myself the love of my life was now my *first* true love. That after nearly four years, there was no more "we." No more Emilly and Dale. No more growing (up) together.

* * *

In the months before my 21st birthday, there were many things worthy of celebration in my life. I had graduated with a B.A.—the second in my family—early and with honors. I earned a minor worth more credits than some majors. I made it to my twenties without ever getting pregnant. I was finally talking to a therapist I actually liked. I would get my turn to walk in a college graduation ceremony in front of my whole family.

But every triumph felt so small. I had spent the last semester in school going through the motions of being a student like a zombie bored of chewing skulls. I knew I could no longer be a martyr, a public school teacher. I still hadn't fully shaken the feeling that overwhelmed me after witnessing the long, grueling hours and no support I had only read about before. I knew that was the reality of many teachers, but it was a whole lot grimmer to face when I was in the classroom raking hours for my practicum requirement.

I knew I only had to be there for three months. I also knew if I went through with becoming a teacher, I'd get burned out fast and leave a graduate program with another handful of zeros added to my student debt. So instead, I became a robot one semester away from graduation, writing papers and showing up while consumed by the feeling of having just spent the past three years working 32 hours a week amid full course loads, just to end up on another path towards nothing.

I didn't want to be back in the Bay for my 21st birthday. This was the first time being back home for the summer without Dale. The first time coming back since we left for Portland right after my 18th birthday. The first time since we packed our bags eager to start the next chapter of our lives together as high school-turned-college sweethearts. But I needed to be back in the Bay to make money and I needed some time away from Portland to focus on getting better.

* * *

That summer in California felt like I was in the exact same place I was when I was 16 years old. I was working at the same private summer school in Menlo Park—albeit while house-sitting for David Byrne's former personal assistant in East Palo Alto instead of living at my mom's. I also felt like I'd regressed right back into my personal teenage girldom: single, depressed, and with the anorexic tendencies of my first years of high school back in charge, holding the reigns. The urgency to feel flaca, to feel skinny had, once again, taken control of my body and brain even though I thought I had learned to quell it.

When I was alone, I'd look at old pictures of me and Dale. I'd feed my impulse to click through my Facebook albums on full screen and pause to study: the lines around Dale's eyes, the curvature of his right arm around my shoulders, the gingham black dress I no longer fit into. I looked at the photos and wondered how I could have thought I, we, were anything but perfect then. I looked at myself in the mirror and grasped at my belly, wondering how I could have let myself look like *this* now. Part of me knew it was fucked up and that my thoughts were the stupid regurgitation of a society that convinces people to hate their bodies. Part of me couldn't stop the thoughts from coming, no matter how hard I tried. I couldn't stop comparing.

When Dale and I were together, I was eventually eating regularly. I got back into cooking elaborate meals and I thought I had shaken anorexia for good, even though I was never treated. Then the break-up with Dale sent me into another spiral after three years of thinking I was good. I wasn't exclusively grazing on celery sticks or eating a half-cup of cottage cheese with four strawberries for dinner, but I started this bout by returning to skipping breakfast altogether again.

"I don't get hungry until at least three hours after I wake up," I'd say. I pretended, again, not to know I was doing it on purpose.

I have always been good at lying to myself. I didn't know starving myself, neglecting myself was a key ingredient in my unraveling.

I thought all I needed to believe in was that I had the will to get better, just like my mom taught me. I just had to force myself to swallow food. I just had to force myself to eat enough meals each day. I just had to force myself to get out of bed each morning. I thought it was just a simple choice, all my own.

* * *

I had quit working at Buffalo Exchange hastily, one month before my college graduation. I was fed up with the micro-management and suburban high school-level cattiness of their management. I thought it might be nice to be unemployed and work on creative projects, but I burned through my savings faster than I expected. It turns out it's a lot harder to keep to a routine when you don't *need* to. It's also hard to get started on anything creative when you're caught up feeling like a wannabe creative person—like a stone-faced phony-ass fraud. Unemployment was another key ingredient to my unraveling. It was also a key ingredient to the crumbling of my self-worth and this cycle of regression.

In my two months without a job or a boyfriend, I stumbled deeper into my depression and self-destructive ways. Skipping one meal a day led to two. I walked miles and miles each day, having sold my car when I came to Portland and losing access to a car when I was dumped. I learned I could supplement my hunger (and sometimes my sadness) with cans of beer and Jack Daniel's straight from the bottle. When I knew I was going to smoke weed—which was just about every night—I skipped two meals to account for the inevitable munchies. I tried so hard to keep up with my much punker friends.

Then I stayed awake for 48 hours straight for the first time in my life celebrating my friend Melanie's April birthday. Somewhere, around hour thirty-five, we went to Sauvie Island. I looked out the windows at the open fields we were passing by on our drive. I thought about how Melanie had recently told me she had to fight back random gory visions. The most recent one was when she was in our shared Clinton Street kitchen chopping baby carrots. Melanie told me she had spaced out to the steady, rocking sound of the blade hitting the bamboo board beneath. When she looked down, she saw the bloody nubs of her fingers in place of carrots for a split-second. So, she closed her eyes for a moment. Took a breath, then reopened them. She found her fingers were still attached. She didn't feel particularly relieved.

In the small SUV we were crammed into, I looked from the fields to Melanie as she opened up the car's sunroof. She put her body through the opening, closed her eyes, and swayed slowly, back-and-forth, with her arms raised. The gold necklace beneath her black lace shirt glimmered. I thought *this is exactly what being young and alive and free in your 20s is supposed to look like*. Then I pictured a violent, fiery car crash. I saw us dead, tumbling inside the SUV as it rolled over and over in slow motion.

I thought it was a premonition. I really believed I had the power to see the future. I put on my seat belt and told my friends to do the same.

* * *

The months of living recklessly—of living just like a liberated punk rock feminist woman should—were starting to grind me down. I was having a ball. My friends and I were partying every night. When they snorted bumps of cocaine, I stuck to weed and booze, and still felt like I had to keep up. The first guy I slept with as a single-for-the-first-time-adult was the drummer of a band I had a huge crush on for years. We were both wasted and rolled around a twin bed in the closet-turned-fifth bedroom of a house I used to live in. He promised me he'd give me drum lessons for the new Pearl drum set I'd bought off Craigslist, for free. I couldn't believe how sexy I suddenly thought arm muscles were.

Then after me and the drummer, I kept learning how I could, somewhat easily, get with more guys in bands or random guys at bars. How I'd come out of this four-year relationship *hot*. How I could also accidentally get with some hot weirdos, like the also-wasted dude who fell asleep in the 5AM cab ride on the way over to his apartment. He had a poster of "niña con máscara de calavera" (Girl with Death Mask)—the same obscure-ish Frida Kahlo painting I had tattooed on my arm. He told me, cigarette dangling in his mouth indoors, his ex-girlfriend had given it to him as a gift. (This wasn't the quickest a guy I was hooking up with told me about his ex). We laid on the mattress plopped in the center of the west side studio apartment, sun coming in through the blinds. Then he brrrrr'd his lips while eating me out, blowing slobbery raspberries like a loud ass vacuum cleaner in pursuit of my pleasure, only to fall asleep mid-suck.

I also had my first real, intense make-you-grin-until-your-cheeks-fall-off crush on another woman. I started to see the dots between the things I thought *normal straight girls did* and how maybe, next to each other, they might mean something different. Like how I'd grown to prefer porn without men, and solo scenes, and assumed other straight girls did too. Like how I figured everyone went through a phase fantasizing about hooking up and holding hands with other girls and being afraid of what it might mean to tell our families. I also thought how maybe it was a little bit different if the girls you tended to like were androgynous, and how it didn't really count unless you'd gone *all the way*. Right? And how I'd still think, for many years, I was just straight on account of my dating history. How maybe this stretch of intense crushes was just me being crazy. How when I confided in my aunt's girlfriend I was starting to identify as queer, she suggested I keep telling people I was straight because girls like me—girls who are down to go any which way the wind blows—make it harder for lesbian femmes, and easier for men to suggest they just need a good dick to set them straight. And I wouldn't want my openness to any gender, while in a relationship with another cis man, to take up any space or take away from what others experience. So, I would try to ignore my fantasies of connections being realized, of what may have been if I went *all the way* in my early twenties. At least out loud to my family. Eventually I will come out, in writing, on Twitter each year on #BiVisibilityDay, and maybe also tucked deep into a book I write.

* * *

I knew I should be doing more with my life—more creative work, but I didn't know where or how to shift my focus. *Focusing* felt out of reach even when I actively tried.

My brain and life started to fog. It was like everything was moving too fast, but I'd have moments I began calling "vibes" when my mind told me the world was moving in slow motion. I saw everything around me, for short bursts, like my very own Marvel movie, slowed to 0.5x. I gained the confidence of Black Widow when I saved a lost pug after seeing it sprint down Rosa Parks Way and having the dexterity for a swift pick up. I could sense when someone was about to talk to me. I thought everyone was dying to talk to me. I could cut through the bullshit and detect what people were really thinking—the true intentions behind empty words. I thought I really knew everyone. I thought this higher way of being was my destiny.

Then on the evening of Tupac Shakur's birthday, I had an idea: I was going to start a new blog! I tried to write down my many fleeting thoughts. I wrote a blog post called "HAPPY BDAY PAC!!!!!" and said my clinically-depressed-ass had found a way to finally be *happy*. I said it was all because I'd found my calling. I'd found my purpose. I knew my path.

I had also just slept with a new dreamboat who told me I was *beautiful*.

I had also only slept three hours that night.

I felt like I was on top of the world.

I didn't know what time it was. Time was a construct. I wrote for hours about my grand idea: *I'll interview people about their lives!*

I searched for the domain name I wanted and purchased it. I proceeded to tell all of Facebook about it. I shuffled between my 50 open tabs. But my 74 WPM typing was no match for my avalanche of racing thoughts: *Must create Twitter. Must create an Instagram. Must write about it on Tumblr. Must create a BUZZ. Must email the media!*

I took a nap for two hours and woke up knowing I felt off. I scoured WebMD and took a self-screener for ADHD. I cycled between thinking something was happening that maybe shouldn't and, in that moment, with my many matching symptoms, I decided ADHD must certainly be what was *wrong* with me. I cried at the news of my new diagnosis, my new answer, my new solution. I cried because I felt like this might be the last hurdle I'd been looking to overcome my whole life—the last thing standing in my way of feeling different. The last thing I needed to be strong through, so I could finally reach a life that was normal.

Then I got back to business post-ADHD diagnosis. I identified twelve admirable Portlanders as my first interview subjects. I wrote a vague and erratic email to "the original 12" telling them about my plans to become a world-famous journalist and civil rights leader. My mind continued to race. I couldn't believe I was on the verge of starting a movement.

I tried to capture all my thoughts in a blog post: *This is it! This is what I want to do with my life. The universe, or God herself, is beaming down my direction. Shoot, why should I settle for people in Portland? How about people all over the world? We just need unity! There is so much violence and hurt in the world. We need to lift up regular people! We need togetherness! Everyone has a story! Everyone has a voice! That voice should be heard! I'll be the one to help their voices be heard! Must email the mayor. Must email the president. Must email Afeni Shakur, Tupac's mom. Must create buzz. Must create a movement.*

My big idea became even bigger, became inflated. My social media posts documented the ballooning. I tweeted at celebrities about the #NewCivilRightsMovement I was leading. I took selfies and captioned them, "The Face of a Revolutionary." I wrote poems. I wrote a manifesto. This was all happening within 24 hours. **I could not stop.**

My unraveling came to a head the next morning after I published a series of YouTube videos. The one that made people start to message me was a video I recorded at 4AM where I was listening to "Changes" by 2Pac and crying.

"Emilly, you're not making any sense," one message read.

"Umm. . . what are you talking about?" said another.

"Hey, don't take this the wrong way, but are you alright?"

I wondered if I was. I called my mom at 7AM and asked her point blank: "Mom, am I crazy?"

She told me all I needed was to get some rest. I deleted the videos and asked an angel of a new friend named Amy to come over to help me.

Amy fed me two pink Benadryl pills and scrubbed my social media clean while I slept. We ate breakfast at a nearby diner and I swapped quickly between laughter and streams of tears. I couldn't even finish eating my breakfast. Picking up a fork was hard. I didn't know how long we'd been sitting, but I think it was a very long time. She drove me to the nearest hospital when I told her I needed help for real. Amy sat with me in urgent care, and we talked shit about the snarky, judgy intake nurse when she left us in the waiting room. Amy told me not to worry. She'd seen this before. Mania. She promised me I'd be okay.

* * *

I spent the next four days admitted to the emergency psychiatric ward of a hospital. I spent the four days leading up to my college graduation terrified, perpetually unsure of my surroundings and the complexity of how I'd arrived. The emergency psych ward is like a sterilized hospital holding cell made just for patients with immediate needs—to be watched, evaluated, and stabilized (most frequently following suicide attempts).

I got knocked out cold for the first 24 hours with Geodon; an antipsychotic, a standard procedure. The additional three days were spent talking to different strangers about my *symptoms* and *stressors* and *trauma*. I got even more sick of therapists dredging up shit I didn't want to think or talk about. I spent each day trying new elixirs of meds to correct—er, *nurture*—my brain's newly discovered chemical imbalance. The chemical imbalance wasn't new—it had always been there—but my recent recklessness had finally caused it to emerge.

I learned I was suffering from Bipolar Disorder I. I learned what I experienced was a major mixed-state episode—"a dangerous combination of mania and depression." I learned all of the radical, liberating, feminist, punk things I did in the months leading up to this moment fed my unraveling: the alcohol, the marijuana, the lack of sleep, the abundance of sex, the starvation. These all fed my body's inability to regulate my mood, fed all sides of my extremes, and awakened my dormant disorder.

I learned I am *mentally ill*. I learned there is no cure for my craziness. I learned I'll never truly be *normal*. I became further skeptical of myself, and of a future.

My days became blurred and stretched. Time remained incomprehensible: there were no clocks in the psych ward except a single digital one that occupied the space beneath the glass windows where various hospital workers converged to observe and speculate each patients' unique brand of crazy. I remember thinking I might feel better if the observation tower was made using two-way mirrors like the ones in *Law and Order: SVU*. At least then it would give the illusion of privacy. Instead, they watched each of us closely and pretended they didn't see us—a calculated and precise balance of being stalked yet also invisible.

Every day we'd check a white board for our "suggested" daily schedule. We were told routines would help. The regular offerings of morning meditation, free meals, lessons in wellbeing, and art therapy made it sound like an expensive new age resort, but the outlandish cost was the only similarity.

During hospital visiting hours, my family brought me organic fruit because patients weren't allowed to receive flowers.

I didn't let my mom come in the first day because I was too embarrassed to let her see me, and also too mad from all the childhood memories that had been coming back to me in therapy. I was afraid of looking into her eyes and seeing them filled with disappointment, sadness, or worse—pity. When I gave my mom the green light to visit on day three, I promised her I'd "get better" in time to get out for graduation.

Art therapy hour was my favorite. We'd use dull crayons and stubby felt-tip markers to doodle aimlessly which sounds sad, but it wasn't. I'd sit with other patients and take my pick from the perforated coloring book mandalas and zone out. We'd listen to Fleetwood Mac's *Rumours* which was a win, but we'd also have to listen to our therapist's many warnings of the ways we might become "repeat offenders." I thought "repeat offenders" was a perfect word to describe the blend of criminalization and institutional imprisonment we, mentally ill folks, were facing there, beyond our own minds. I knew my situation—my access to family and health care and money—wasn't the same. I knew I had to listen to the therapist and hospital workers, even though I didn't feel ready to change and give up my whole way of life. I felt like I was back in college zombie mode—best to stick to the motions and try to get out quickly.

On day four, Erika talked to the doctors about my diagnosis and hospital protocol. We learned the 5150—the psychiatric hold that gives the hospital temporary legal authority to keep people in who are thought to seriously be at risk of hurting themselves or others—had lapsed after my first 48 hours. I decided I felt stable enough to get out. I signed a giant stack of papers and discharged myself the evening before graduation.

* * *

I stayed in Embassy Suites that night with my family. I sewed a pocket on the inside of my graduation gown like I'd done when

I completed high school, so I could keep my cell phone and pills within easy reach. In line to enter the Rose Garden arena where I would graduate, I popped a half pill of Ativan to keep my intense anxiety at bay. I sat in the center of the arena for four hours with my classmates. I kept the other half-pill tucked in my pocket in the event of an emergency. I could barely keep my eyes open, but I was able to walk across the stage with a toothy smile. The announcer said my name in the nasally "Pray-dough" mispronunciation. I was pissed that I'd busted my ass for that moment, but I was there and that's mostly all that mattered to me.

After the ceremony, I held flowers that my Papi and sister, Daniela, brought in one arm. I held the ones my mom and stepdad picked out, along with ones from my sister, Erika, in the other. I wondered if any of these flowers were originally destined for the hospital. I thought both were worth celebrating.

After graduation dinner, I felt the mania creeping back up in our hotel room. The rapid thoughts, the unsteadiness. I was still so afraid. I tried to keep the crying to myself then took the second half of my Ativan and asked Erika to take care of me. She rubbed my back. She big spooned me until we both fell asleep.

11. nothing came out

THE FIRST TIME I knew I loved Dale was before we were together. When we both transferred from our respective high schools to the tiny community-college-instead-of-high-school alternative program as juniors, he was still dating a girl named Juniper who he'd grown up with at their letter-gradeless granola nursery-to-eighth-grade private school. I knew he was in a three-year relationship when we met. I was in the middle of a two-year relationship of my own. His girlfriend wore ankle length skirts and smiled closed-mouth smiles in family pictures on his mom's Facebook page. Juniper was wholesome, pretty, and seemed nice, even though I thought she was a bit mousy. I was still dating Damien. Dale was my crush.

When Dale told our group of friends at school one day that he was going through a breakup, I hoped he would be okay. For a second my heart danced thinking we might get to be together, but then I realized I didn't know who'd done the breaking up with yet. I cared so much about him; I wanted his heart to remain whole above everything else—even if that meant him choosing her over me. I hoped they'd get back together so his heart wouldn't be broken. The thought felt weird, but also rational. Then I learned he was the one who'd done the dumping. I learned being rational might also be a way to love. We dated—had our own chance to grow up together—for nearly four years.

* * *

I started journaling again, online at a private Blogspot domain. I'd learned the Internet and anonymity were a safer place to keep my secrets. The shadows of my search history were less likely than a hardcover diary to be rifled through.

In September of 2012, shortly after my crazy, and our breakup, I revisited a list I made that March of things I, newly-single, missed. I found that I still missed them just the same (being in love, sleeping in someone's arms, having someone to have sex with on the regular, having someone to spoon at night, having someone to talk with about my day, having someone to tell about my dreams, having someone kiss me on my forehead, on my neck, on my cheek, on my lips. Having someone. Smiling . . .).

So, I wrote a letter to my ex-boyfriend Dale to tell him that I missed him. It had been six months since we officially broke up, seven months if you counted our failed attempt at a "break." Five months of trying to be friends. Three months past the crazy, and what would have been our four-year anniversary. I didn't tell him I was still counting. I sent the letter via SMS. It took him six days to reply.

Dear Emilly,

I apologize that it took me this long to write back to you.

I really appreciate you're being honest about how you feel, and I am going to write an honest response that you deserve. I don't share the same feelings about us. Of course I miss things about our relationship. I also think about our relationship often, and there's plenty of things I miss about being with you—having someone to talk to always, making jokes no one else would get, taking care of each other, having great sex.

However, I still believe that we cannot be in a relationship, because we want different things. Different things make us happy. At the end of our relationship, I found myself pretending to make you happy which is a total dick move (and I'm really sorry still). I'm not yet ready to be in a relationship again (with you or anybody) because I haven't figured out what I want—also I'm burnt out on having the responsibilities of a relationship, and thus I would be a shitty boyfriend.

I don't think it is in vain that you wrote to me, because it is important that we be honest about how we feel. Especially since we are still a part of each other's lives. You haven't ruined our friendship by writing me—I'm glad you're being honest. I totally understand if you're not ready for a friendship. I may not be either because, being attracted to you still, it makes it difficult to be friends. But I'm willing to try and be friends at any point.

We were together for almost four years, and you have been a hugely important part of my life that I am grateful for. I truly care about you and will always care about you.

With Love,
Dale

I read the letter in the bathroom stall in the final hour of a country club childcare shift. I thought I knew he probably didn't feel the same way, and I shed a single tear after looking at his words, crisp pixels, on my phone screen.

I was surprised that I felt something like *happy*. Content. I knew that I needed to move on, and that we'd never get back together. This chapter of my life had, indeed, come to a close.

I think this is what closure feels like.

I was saddened our relationship had become broken beyond repair . . . that no matter how much I cared, or missed him, or thought about it—there was nothing left to be done. The ship of what was the possibility of a life together had sunk.

I was tired of hurting and feeling sad, but a part of me had still been holding onto the idea that this stretch of us apart might just need patience to persevere.

I learned I was ready to move on. Be done. Be healed.

This was the second time I knew I would always love Dale and that us not being together was something I'd be okay with.

12. not ready to make nice

"THEY SAY TIME heals everything, but I'm still waiting" —The Chicks (FKA Dixie Chicks)

I wanted to write an essay about how surviving one sexual assault made me stronger. Strong enough to prevent another sexual assault only a few years later. I wanted to write about how even though victims should never be held responsible, I held my own and I was braver the second time around. I wanted to write how I knew better and learned through trial (optimism) and error (assault).

This bootstraps narrative feels like an easy storyline to aspire to because it is logical, *uplifting,* and does a good job at convincing others our fear can simply be conquered! The bootstraps story is about moving on, moving past, moving upwards, but my story will never be about bootstrapping. My story is not simple nor easy nor resolved by just being *strong*.

* * *

In the Fall of 2012, I became an intern at *Bitch Media* when I was 21. It was still a mostly white feminist staff and transitioning towards being a Black and brown feminist staff too. Our latest issue, *Micro/Macro*, housed my second pair of freelance pieces in its glossy pages. I was damn proud of my two music reviews, written in snappy one-hundred-word bursts. About how those notes made me feel. About how the drum arrangements and boom-thumps of the bass made me want to move. I had zero musical credibility, stayed Googling various instrument noises to confirm the sources of their sound, but my editor assured me all that mattered was that I could really write the way I felt.

At the *Micro/Macro* issue release party—my bipolar-aversary, hordes of writers and attendees huddled around picnic tables, fixated on the thin magazine pages and trivia night handouts, squinting hard to read the answers they jotted down, barely illuminated by the glow of string lights. My trivia team of fellow strangers reveled in the new summer heat as we recounted every instance we could of sexism, misogynoir, and revolution in media. Our sun-starved arms and thighs, newly exposed in shorts and tanks, were close and sometimes stuck together with sweat.

Winning trivia at the Bitch Media party meant an entire free vegetarian pizza, and I was a recent college graduate, broke, and hungry. By the third 30-minute trivia round, lowballs of Bulleit whiskey had begun to sweat alongside our skin, and my second Tecate was halfway empty.

I don't remember the other strangers except one: Herman, a wiry, self-identified feminist hipster, balding at a rate I could only imagine was premature. As I leaned in to get a better look at the trivia questions waiting to be answered for double points, a rogue splinter lodged itself in my thigh. I let out a yelp. Herman wryly offered to help unstick the prick with one eyebrow raised above his horn-rimmed glasses. It could have been creepy, but his charm convinced me otherwise. I will later see this charm as a tactic, not charm as a trait, but I wasn't too experienced with telling the difference yet. I had only been single for a handful of months after my four years of love—at that point, having just ended, still felt like a failure. Our group lost the trivia round, and I lost my pizza. But after the release party, Herman and I continued lively conversations about youth activism and the fight for free healthcare.

We headed to the bar next door for tall cans of Rainier and virtual Big Buck animal killing sprees. The shooting felt all wrong, but I figured it was just because I was vegetarian. We fired more shots and plunged some pinballs. A few more hours passed. We tossed back draft pints of PBR. Last call was coming up soon.

As we readied to leave, the environmental do-gooder repeatedly complained about having to bike to North Portland after drinking so much booze. We were on the central east side; it probably wouldn't have taken him more than a twenty-minute ride but drinking and biking was dangerous. I had stopped a whole beer before him. I told him he could catch a ride with me and crash on my couch. He smiled and kissed me from the passenger seat right when we got in the car. "We're not having sex," I said, trying on my latest iteration of sexually liberated feminist bravado. *Consent* meant open communication according to an article I'd read in *Bitch*.

Herman leaned over, both of us strapped into my icy blue hoopty, for another make out session before the drive over. Ten minutes later, we pulled up to my apartment. Its exterior paint was peeling back and, inside, it had a thick oatmeal carpet with a strong 1970s vibe, and not in a cute way.

We sat in the living room for a while and he asked if I was really going to make him sleep on the couch. I said yes. He said no, but in a shifty, jokey way. We did this, back and forth, yes and kinda-no, a few more times.

"We're not going to have sex," I said to Herman in my living room after I agreed to let him sleep in my bed. He was 6'2" after all, and I didn't want to come off as a *bitch*.

"We're not going to have sex," I said again in my bedroom upstairs.

"We're not going to have sex," I said again as he laid next to me in bed.

"We're not going to have sex," I said again as he started kissing me in my bed.

I thought it again as he moved his hand past my underwear.

I thought it again as he shoved his fingers in my vagina while saying, "Is this okay?"

I thought it again as I didn't answer.

I thought it again as my mind left my body behind.

We're not going to have sex.

I was a broken record on repeat.

I was not a woman with autonomy or a voice. Then my throat stopped working. Time became unrecognizable. Time dragged on and was nauseatingly long. I was stuck, frozen.

After he finished, he fell asleep. *We're not going to have sex*, I repeated in my head until I fell asleep too.

* * *

The next morning, the 21-year-old (me) drove the 24-year-old (him) back to his house in North Portland. We made small talk through gritted teeth about the rest of our weekend plans and how nice it was that the sun was coming out more again. I swore the insides of my 1999 Honda Civic were closing in on us; a boa constrictor gleefully squeezing until we suffocated. I kept my eyes on the road while Herman talked. I didn't know what to say, or which of my cycling feelings were the realest—anger, confusion, smallness, wanting approval. I didn't know what words might explain why I was still driving him home, or why exactly it felt wrong.

He instructed me to slow my moderately-dented ride to an indigo Victorian bungalow.

"Welp. . . thanks for the ride," the man waved from his seat, clutching the door handle as the sedan idled.

"No problem," I said.

There was apparently no longer a need for niceties or charm. There was no need for promises neither of us intended to keep, even though part of me still wanted him to want me. Maybe a phone number request would have made me felt like I wasn't just a body. Maybe then I wouldn't have felt so easily used and discarded. Something felt off, weird, but I couldn't quite place what it was. I wrote him a message on OKCupid to tell him he should listen to women—that I had *told* him we weren't going to have sex—and what he had done had caused me harm.

On the bus ride back from a bar one night soon after, the tequila pulled my dormant tears out and onto my cheeks. The drops of water glimmered underneath the magenta and butterscotch TriMet lights, and I tucked my knees into my chest firmly occupying the last row. I whispered each and every detail to my friend Aubrie who listened and didn't interrupt. I didn't know why I was feeling so bent out of shape by rejection.

My rubber band throat pulled and stretched and snapped as I tried to make sense of an evening that made no sense at all. *How come I kept saying no and how come it didn't work? Why did my body betray me even after I had said no? Why couldn't I move and shove him off? Why was I frozen and turned on and terrified all at once? Why didn't he stop when I said no? Why the fuck did everything about this feel so fucking wrong?*

I chipped away the stubborn layer of black Wet n' Wild nail polish that had clung to my thumb nail for far too long. It was easier to watch the flakes of dried chemicals fall to my lap than to look directly at my friend, her eyes assaulting me with sympathy and love and more pity than I could bear.

Weeks later, on that same bus line, Herman jogged by and we locked eyes as the bus turned a corner. All I could do was give him the nastiest, dirtiest look of my life, protected by a window. I wished my eyes could shoot daggers and leave him to bleed out on the concrete. He had most definitely read my message at that point, telling him what he did to me was wrong and not okay. I found him online days after, but he still hadn't responded— couldn't be bothered to take time away from his social justice organizing day job or fake radical Twitter followers. I felt puke rage and thrash about in my stomach, begging to be let out.

* * *

Six tattoos, eighteen bylines, nineteen new pounds, and one failed yearlong relationship later, I met Curtis. He was the first person I matched with during another bout of endless Tinder swiping and forced romantic optimism. Curtis was another modern-day wolf in sheep's (or Urban Outfitters) clothing.

This time, I was 24 years old. He said he was 27 years old. He pretended to ride the roof of a car like a surfboard in his picture, pixels just small enough and camera shot just far away enough to obscure the true fuckability of his face. After some witty words were exchanged, I deemed him worthy of judging in real life.

Curtis showed great enthusiasm via those gray Tinder text bubbles, asking me out promptly. "When?" I asked. "ASAFP," he said. I appreciated his bluntness—no waffling or beating around the bush—and I was the flattered recipient of said enthusiasm. He called me gorgeous and said I sounded real smart. A few days later, we agreed to play arcade games together at Ground Kontrol.

I ordered a tall can of PBR at the neon-lit bar before weaving my way through the crowd of mostly men to find Curtis. He would be on the ground level playing pinball, he said. When I found him, his eyes were narrowed in on the tiny silver ball being hurled through the playfield by his flippers.

Curtis was tall in real life, towering a full foot above me. His spirit may have been youthful in pixel form, but his face was not. He didn't look old exactly, but he did not look 27. His skin was weathered, his Adam's apple was pronounced. He looked like a "man," hard stop. Not even someone you'd call "young man."

I went in for a handshake and he went in for a hug. He was a self-proclaimed "touchy-feely guy." I tried not to grimace when he said this and didn't tell him as someone who had grown up with minimal hugs and words of affirmation, I was most definitely not. Past Tinder dates also thought the handshakes I offered were awkward, but I preferred them to waving hello in close proximity.

I waded through less than thirty minutes of small talk before asking him how old he really was. He curled the fingers on his right hand and gnawed on his knuckles, pretending to bite down. He sheepishly smiled, looking down into the hallow pit in the Creature from the Black Lagoon pinball game and right back up at me, past my eyes.

"Is it that obvious?" he asked.

I smiled, said nothing, and waited for a reply.

"Thirty-seven," he said, blurting out how Tinder was linked to Facebook and he couldn't change his birthday because of it.

When I offered suggestions for fixing the error, he said his friend had done it and he didn't have the password. It didn't add up, but I wasn't ready to totally abandon this bout of optimism yet.

Curtis played by his own rules. He told me how much he liked me. He wildly hip-checked pinball machines, daring them to tilt. He ran his right hand from the peak of my shoulder down to my fingertips. He told me, only three drinks in, he wanted me to be his girlfriend. He didn't believe in boundaries.

After a few rounds of beers and pinball, Curtis suggested we head to a hip bar in Northeast Portland for nachos. I offered him a ride over since he had taken the bus. He held my face in his hands when he kissed me outside before heading over. I hadn't been kissed by anyone in months.

We found booth seats at the next bar and Curtis kept trying to hold my hand across the table. He was loud and fond of absurdity, dancing in line to the Biggie tracks the DJ played and giddily egging on our booth neighbors to guess how long we had known each other. I felt equal parts mortification and flattery. They guessed about a year.

At bar number two, Curtis had drained two full pints while I sipped on mine. It was getting late and he was noticeably drunk. I was tired and had to work early the next morning. He offered another round, but I counter-offered with a ride home. He accepted. Before getting into my car, we kissed again.

We both lived relatively close to the bar. The drive to my house would have been about fifteen minutes and Curtis said his house was less than ten. I told him to put on his seat belt and I turned over the engine. He kissed me again, only this time his hand moved from my jawline to gripping my throat, a little too tightly. I pulled back. I felt the hairs on my neck stand straight up.

Then it was like the spark of the engine ignited Curtis's sense of urgency. His own engine revved from zero to 100 and my pulling back stood in the way of what he wanted. Curtis's hand moved from my shoulder to my knee as I drove. I pushed it away as he neared my skirt. I idled at a red light and he reached over his seat to kiss my neck some more—he didn't have to lean very far on account of his stature. His face was covered in my lipstick. Every touch felt heavier than the last. I writhed as my body was touched, trying to focus on speeding to his house to make it all stop, while smiling politely. He tried to turn my head with his hands, but I didn't want to kiss him back.

I slowed on his street. He lived on a block of well-manicured lawns in a bougie, *Stepford Wives* neighborhood. His house was the only one with the porch light on. I stopped in front of his neighbor's driveway, keeping the car on, and said goodnight. He smiled and said he'd had such a great night with me.

"Want to come inside and watch a movie?" he asked.

I said no—I had to work early. I'd be waking up in just a few hours. He explained I could sleep over, too.

"Just come in," he said. "It will be fun."

"What? You don't like movies?"

"Come on. You know you want to."

"I want you to come inside so we can have sex!"

"It will be easy," he said.

"It will be easy," he said again and again.

He raised his voice and promised me he'd call me the next day and he wouldn't disappear, so if that's what I was worried about, I didn't have to worry anymore.

"*Don't worry.* This won't be a one-time thing."

I couldn't tell him I worried that he wouldn't get out of my car. I was worried he'd use his 6'3" frame to pick me up out of the driver's seat. I was worried about all the things that might go wrong—that I might attempt to use my mace in this enclosed space out of desperation, that I might hold down my car horn and honk, hoping a rich white stranger might be brave enough to venture outside (even though I knew I'd probably still be left all alone). I was worried about the scenes playing out inside my head but, most of all, I was worried that I'd give in to going inside and have my firm Nos ignored again.

I repeated that I had to go home. My voice felt so far away. I was frozen again.

"I have to go home," I said.

I stared straight ahead and stopped speaking, heart pumping violently. I kept my hands on the steering wheel to keep them from shaking.

Curtis went back down to zero. His shout softened to a theatrically melancholy murmur. He told me I made him feel really sad. *He was so vulnerable with me and I had broken his heart.* His shoulders slouched. He dropped his head. Then he languidly pushed his door open. With one foot on the ground, he paused and turned to look into my eyes. I imagined him dead. He pretended to be pained, then got out and closed the door behind him. My foot slammed straight down onto the pedal like I'd seen in movies.

I got away, but I did not feel strong.

I tried to breathe. Tears immediately flooded my eyes, making my face hot and wet. I cried the entire way home. I cried as I washed my face, scrubbing the lipstick down the drain. I cried as I put on my pajamas and cried until I fell asleep, thinking that no matter how hard of a feminist game I talked, I was still just a weak woman.

I called out of work the next morning. I made myself mint tea and drew a hot bath. I tried to read the autobiography of Assata Shakur as an empowering distraction:

> *"Over and over they would tell me, 'You're as good as anyone else. Don't let anybody tell you that they're better than you. . . Don't respect nobody that don't respect you, you hear me?' 'Yes, Grandmother,' I would answer, my voice almost a whisper. 'Speak up!' she would tell me repeatedly."*
> —Assata Shakur

I cried again.

* * *

Curtis sent me 17 texts the next day begging me to go on another date. He blamed the alcohol for trying to force me into his house. He unmatched me on Tinder somewhere around his tenth text. I told him he didn't understand boundaries and I blocked his number. I reported him on Tinder, and they said they'd look into it, but couldn't provide updates out of "respect" for Curtis's privacy. I never received any updates.

Weeks passed before I could answer the phone again at work. I had been working as a customer service rep at a toxic tech company and my job was to save people, mid-vacation or business trip, from things like grime-covered toilets at $49 per night Coachella festival apartments, or being locked out, at 3AM, of the castle they'd rented in rural Spain. I had become so afraid the person on the other end might yell at me that I avoided answering the line altogether. I tried making our stringent quota of closed cases by cherry-picking our email inbox instead. I deleted Tinder and then redownloaded and did this a few more times.

A few months after the attempted assault, I went on a date with a sweet, stylish greaser babe with Lotería tattoos, a pickup truck, and his own vintage-adorned apartment. We knocked down pins at a now-demolished bowling alley. I flinched when he grazed my hand, reaching for his bowling ball. I sat across from him at a restaurant when he offered to let me sit on his side of the booth to look at the nice view outside together. The new guy asked me twice if I was okay during our first date, and twice again when he served me wild mushrooms sautéed in brown butter and sage over pasta on our second date. He said I seemed distracted. I wanted to tell him the fear of men, of being assaulted or almost assaulted, had followed. I wanted to tell him I wanted to feel present. I wanted to tell him I thought at another point in time we might've had a future. But all we had together was two dates, and one cordial kiss. It was all too soon.

* * *

I kept trying to move on, but sexual trauma is a grief and a ghost—still alive in your bones, dormant until a certain touch or look or place or noise or reminder reawakens it. It never feels truly done or over or gone.

I tried to convince myself everything should be okay; *I narrowly escaped. I made it out. This was different.* But deep down I knew that even though Curtis hadn't succeeded in forcing me into his bed, he certainly could have overpowered me with his size if he really wanted. He could have made me do things I didn't want to. Go places I didn't want to go. He reminded me my safety was never really in my own hands. My safety was dependent on him.

I didn't know how to talk to my old friends Aubrie and Melanie about what had happened. Getting alone time and space to get deep with them was less easy and frequent than ever. I turned to new friends who'd also been assaulted. They told me about an online community for people like us named after mythical, misunderstood goddesses.

It took this secret Facebook group for sexual assault survivors, dozens of likes on a confessional post I made about language use and what happened with Curtis and Herman, and one specific commenter's written permission for me to say the word *rape* about my own experience. I had readily encouraged anyone else with a similar story to mine—the "grayness," we are told, of losing touch with our bodies in the middle of an assault—to use *rape* if they wanted, but I struggled to say *rape* on my own for a very long time. I stuck to only saying *rape* to my online community and friends for many more years to come. I never told any cops.

Rape is violence and violation. I didn't want to admit to myself that I had been raped. I didn't want to accept that I had been violated—that violation in any form is still always violence—and that my body was taken hostage by somebody else. That my voice was ignored even when I spoke up. That my voice threatened to fail me a second time around. That even though my rape didn't look like the rape on TV, it was still rape.

Being able to say *rape* about Herman happened almost five years after he raped me. It still makes me feel sick with rage to even type "rape."

* * *

In the United States, one in five women will face an attempted or completed rape. Eighty-eight percent of women will experience sexual harassment and/or assault. LGBTQ and BIPOC face disproportionate rates of sexual assault. When #MeToo went viral on Facebook in 2017, I didn't have the courage to out myself as another statistic—another case of my fucked-up luck. I wanted to be brave. I wanted to write my own Facebook post and feel the warmth of supportive comments (the Internet at its best). But I was still in shock. Still too ashamed.

Not long after the movement continued gaining momentum, Sally, a friend from the local activist scene, was hired as the Executive Director of the non-profit where Herman worked. Sally and I were in touch every few months via Facebook where she'd pitch me abortion access fundraisers or pro-union punk shows she was involved in to include in my weekly activism events column for *The Portland Mercury*. I promised myself if she ever asked me for any press coverage in her new position as Herman's boss, I'd decline and tell her why.

Then one day, the DM came from Sally asking if I'd include a blurb about the upcoming student walkout her organization was planning. I politely said no and told her the reason for declining coverage. Conflict of interest: benefitting my rapist. I kept Herman's name anonymous in my initial message but said my assailant had also raped at least one other person I knew. She figured out his name on her own—process of elimination—and I confirmed her suspicions.

An avalanche of Facebook messages followed. The 57-message exchange spanned three weeks. She began, after naming Herman, by asking me how I would like her to respond. *He is planning to leave within the year* was also included in that message. I didn't want to belabor my reply. I didn't give a shit if he was already planning on leaving. I had made myself a promise that I intended to keep. I had already spent so many years trying to protect myself by avoiding thinking or speaking of what he did to me. I told her I'd leave the decision-making to her, as Executive Director, for what was best for her organization, but also mentioned that while he was working there, I'd continue to never be involved or use what small public platform I had to share their work.

I also don't want this to be a public thing, I wrote to her. *I've seen what friends go through who do callouts. I don't want to go through that. I've sat on this for years but promised myself if anyone ever asked me to support [redacted], I'd be transparent.*

I had witnessed a close friend face intense harassment, workplace trolling, and scrutiny after writing her account of a rape that nobody believed, before #MeToo. She wrote her story in response to a post her own rapist published—then deleted—on Facebook which was momentarily lauded as "bravery" when he detailed his horrifying latest attempt at *blacked out* rape with a pseudo apology. While a few publications covered my friend's story with a semblance of respect, most, including *The Daily*

Mail participated in rape culture and slut shaming first-hand, centering the perpetrator and scouring social media to use her thirst traps as a way of insinuating lack of credibility. Uncut footage from a twenty-minute segment of a local NBC affiliate anchor interviewing her rapist was accidentally aired in which the newscaster and cameraman both empathized with their interviewee between takes, naming *him* the victim verbatim. I had also accompanied another friend and held her hand while she recounted, in visceral detail, her own experience of rape to a callous Portland cop. We sat in a frigid interrogation room. He didn't ask many questions beyond, "Why'd you wait so long?"

I told Sally I wanted to stay anonymous. I kept my answers to her subsequent DMs short. I emailed screenshots—a small semblance of evidence where I called Herman coercive via OKCupid and received a reply—as requested. I supplemented my DMs with an article that explained how sexual coercion was not consent, and how a lack of consent is the definition of rape. My friend who had also been raped by Herman, a now-sober former addict, agreed to come forward too. She had been Herman's underage intern when he started "dating" her and buying her many bottles of booze. One day, somewhere between my Herman and Curtis timeline, we came to know we shared a rapist while comparing notes of sexual conquests on our respective iPhones. I used to include a "Douchebag Herman" on mine. I no longer do.

I wanted to share what had been done to us to protect other young girls and women in the future. My friend wanted the same. She agreed to share her own story with the Executive Director. She even agreed to the organization's request for a seven-person conference call when I declined on account of not wanting to rehash my trauma, on account of not wanting to end up sobbing on the phone to a bunch of strangers. I am still in awe of how loudly she was able to use her voice. I am still afraid there is a version of this story where, if I didn't ask my beautiful brave white friend for help—in coming forward with her more horrifying, undeniable account of rape—my story of rape would be deemed unbelievable too.

But Herman *was* fired from his job. I learned this in a two-sentence Facebook message from the Executive Director. I didn't ask for further details. I felt better knowing he couldn't rape others as easily anymore, at least not through his job as a youth policy organizer. I didn't feel much else, but I wanted to. I wanted to feel a sense of relief or of pride for having come forward, but nothing really felt changed or fixed inside.

Justice didn't feel like it was served. I'm still unsure what kind of punishment is the equivalent of leaving a mark on someone else's body and mind forever.

13. in dreams

IN THE HOSPITAL, I hold your cold, stiff hand in my own and try to warm it. The first time I tried, I waited until it was just me and your mom. I only had the nerve to grip a single finger.

An ex-lover-turned-friend should be able to hold your hand if you're dying, but it's not that simple. We haven't spoken in months and the last time you texted I was giddy to take a turn ignoring your words. Last you heard from me, I wanted to get together for one last goodbye before moving back to California. When you texted back two months later, I had already changed my mind but couldn't let you know that.

I didn't know when I'd see you next, but I didn't think it would be with you unconscious in the ICU of Emanuel hospital. The same hospital I had tried to admit myself to during my mental breakdown two years before. Yeah, the same mental breakdown where you let me sleep in your bed with headphones on to try and calm myself in the midst of a manic episode, even though we had been broken up for three months.

Cutting ties with ex-lovers, especially when it hurts, is to be expected and we had also followed suit. Two estranged years is a long time, but so were our four together. How was I supposed to know you'd crash your bike, helmetless, in North Portland? How was I supposed to predict that your family friend, Eliza, would call while I was at my new job and I'd know, in my gut, I should stop what I was doing and answer it? How was I to know you would be found under a bus, having likely slid underneath after drinking too much—but that no one knew for sure? How was I supposed to know you'd be found by strangers on the side of a road? How was I supposed to know we'd maybe never talk again?

* * *

In the hospital room, I am already a ghost. Your old friends and your new friends and your new, whole life without me cycle in and out of the swinging doors. Your accident has made us all change. But I am a relic of the past.

They all call you Miller; I still know you as Dale. They call me a "family friend" because they don't know what else to call me. I don't know what to call myself either. They drink whiskey in cars parked in the lot outside the hospital to give them courage. Their bodies drip in stick-n-poke skulls and machine-inked 8 balls, and they reek of cigarette and spliff chain smoking. It's all to help them feel stronger, but at your bedside, they still crumble, and they cry, and we all cry together.

The room must remain silent save for the mechanism pumping air in and out of your body and the dings that reassure us your heartbeat is still there. For the first two weeks, we wear white hazmat suits and knead hand sanitizer onto our skin until our hands begin to crack.

Your mom slips arnica pills into your mouth when the ICU staff isn't looking. She flew in three hours after getting the call.

Your dad came in two flights later. They stay in Portland for almost half a year.

As I ponder my place in this sterile room, the steady, mechanized beeps transport me to the times we spent at your own sister's bedside, just three years earlier. She was 27 when she died of a cancer. The doctors tell us you won't survive, just as they did with Norina. You are 23. It's surreal sitting in the hospital "family room" again—big desk in between the doctors and us, carpeted floors, whitewashed watercolor art. A room no one knows exists until they need one. A room that exists to lessen the blow of tragedy and pain. Rare brain cancer and traumatic brain injuries are when your family needs them.

In the hallway outside your room, I weep with every ounce of myself into your mother's arms. She holds me like she held you once as a baby. I am soft and malleable, and I can barely stand up. I am ashamed of my need to be taken care of when your family must prepare to strip another child/sibling of the current that pumps life into lungs. I was supposed to surrender access to their love and yours.

Back in your room, I do not feel worthy of holding your hand, of assuming it would be okay to touch any part of a body that is no longer mine, of grasping at connection with a stranger. Strangers who once knew each other long ago.

I think about the time after we broke up for good, when I went in for a hug at the campus bar after a game of indoor soccer. You flinched, shrank back, and offered a few pats on my shoulder instead. You sat four seats away. Why would this time be any different?

Today it is different, though, because the choice is not ours. This could never feel like before and I know there may never be a time that ever feels like before again.

When your hand twitches, so does my heart. The doctors assure me it's an automated reaction from *your body*, not *your brain*. I say I understand.

In a quiet moment without your friends, your anti-tobacco mother asks me if you ever smoked cigarettes. I hesitate by saying your name like a question and choose to lie in allegiance to your secrets. Joints are easier to explain than spliffs anyway. I also don't tell her your heavy drinking was part of our breakup and how maybe I could have stopped all this from happening if I'd just told her, told anyone besides my friends, that I was worried about you before you spiraled. How being tired of caring for you, of rubbing your back while you puked for the entirety of a day, was one of many recurring reasons we were no longer good for each other. How I couldn't really tell the difference between coming of age and binge drinking and alcoholism yet.

While I wonder about my place at your deathbed, I try to grasp onto our sweet memories instead. *5AM cups of coffee in South Carolina.* I jot them down. *Backgammon and Spades in India.* I make lists on my phone. *Taking turns sucking in air while saying "pillow" and "almohada" and laughing so hard until we both cried.* I repeat them in my head on the daily drives over to the hospital and the drives back home. *Watching every obscure Italian horror flick and episodes of* The Sopranos. *Sleeping through a lightning storm camping in Utah and waking up soaked. The time you strummed "Custom Concern" for me on your guitar. The way you'd say you loved me with just your eyes.*

I know that not having you here to share our memories with will make the life we lived together feel even less real. Feel even more far away and spoiled with doubt. Time will work even harder to make sure I forget.

* * *

Above your hospital bed, your buds have pinned up a movie-sized *X-Files* poster that says I WANT TO BELIEVE. Maybe it's about UFOs and aliens, but I need it to mean more than that. I want to believe that our love existed. I want to believe it wasn't all just made up—that it was real and raw and mutual. I want to believe you will get better. I want to believe this isn't the end. I want to believe that if you do die, what we had won't die along with you.

The doctors didn't believe you would get better, but they wanted to believe it was possible. They tried half a dozen surgeries and medications, intent on fighting for the five-percent survival rate they gave you.

Then slowly, somehow, you do get better. Against all odds. Tubes are removed and noise bans are lifted. You can do more than open or blink your eyes. We move you two times in the hospital to different rooms before moving you across town to a dimly lit, depressing in-patient rehab. You graduate to out-patient rehab. Your parents' five-month stay in Portland is up. You get ready to go back home with them, at least until you get as close as you can to one hundred percent better. We try to *move on*.

* * *

One year after the accident, we sit in the same park we sat in as two teenagers madly in love. Still two short blocks from the Menlo Park, California home where you were born. But it's no longer a short walk for a survivor of a TBI.

Despite time, we fall easily into the comfort that comes with knowing a person more closely than anyone else in the world. Your skull has been stitched back together and your darkened hair now hides the scars. Aphasia jumbles your words like the Boggle cubes we used to toss, but you're speaking now. We're speaking. You reach for the word "job" but "cash register" comes out. You reach for the word "Maria," my mother, but "Carlos Santana" comes out.

It takes twenty minutes to work through a conversation that would have taken seconds in our past, but I eagerly soak up the snippets of memories you uncover from your time in the hospital.

I tell you about the sleepless nights roused awake by my body shaking, in tears. How I'd sob in the arms of another boyfriend-turned-ex, mourning for our memories, for your family, and for you. How I'd beg him to hug me until I fell back asleep. How he broke up with me with a cookie cutter line from a movie. How "I can't do this anymore" wasn't the first time I knew that relationship wasn't meant to last.

I try, and fail, to tell you I was afraid of taking up space or holding your hand. How I was worried about being in a place where I may not have been wanted.

"Dream," you say.

And you manage to tell me about the last dream that you had.

You saw me. *I stood stoically on the main deck of a sailing ship, wearing a white gown, in the black of night. A storm was brewing, and the masts trembled terribly, and the sails swung right along with them. I was there, and you were there too.*

But that's all you can remember. Or at least that's all you can muster, sitting next to me here on this California park bench one year later.

Sad, you say of the dream, and it's the last one you've had—the last dream you may ever have because of how your brain is now jumbled. But the dream looped on repeat throughout your coma, keeping you company. Keeping you alive. There was a ship, you say again, and I was there with you.

Words run through my own brain but can't find their way out of my mouth. How can I describe the weight of knowing your last moment on earth could have been spent dreaming of me?

How can I explain I feared our love had been fake? Well, I guess we really did love each other after all.

14. tell it like it is

IT TOOK SIXTEEN minutes for us to be let into the sterile world from the unsterile world. My Tia Lucry, twenty-five years my senior, shifted from right foot to left as we waited for a buzz or a voice or a sign from the other side of the barrier to let us through. I could hear the air between her socks and Sperry Topsiders escape with each tilt of her body, each shrug of her shoulder, each rock from flattened toes to the heels of her feet.

Around minute fourteen, I gave up on staring down the white corded phone on the wall and picked up the receiver again. I held it to my ear. It was still just ringing.

Lucry tried her routine anew: pushing the fiery Lucite red square button to the left of the phone, then tugging on the icy chrome door handle. She tried pulling the boomerang-shaped metal back, but the door boomeranged her body, pulling her in instead. She gave the handle a severe rattling. The door another knock. Nothing.

"I'll try her cell," Lucry said.

I nodded, keeping up the appearance of busy, ear glued to the receiver, waiting for any breaks in its song.

* * *

The drive over to Sequoia Hospital had taken about half as long as the wait to enter the ICU itself. Lucry and I slipped back into our familiar pastime with ease despite a decade spent living in different states. It went like this: Lucry dropped truth bombs between long pauses and red lights, unearthed family secrets, and confirmed and/or denied hypotheses I'd formed most often about my absent father but sometimes about my Mami or a tia or an uncle. We focused on the facts, not feelings.

On this drive, it was Christmas Eve. We warmed up to talking about my Tia Concha, the patient, by discussing my dad. I told her how I'd signed up for Ancestry DNA and wondered when an email would pop into my inbox, confirming the existence of a rumored fourth family in Mexico. More sisters and brothers to add to the roster. She said we didn't need science to prove that. My brain jumped from new siblings to big families to my cousins to our cousin Jose and to his mom, Concha.

Delfina for long, Conch for extra short. She was in the hospital again—too many times over the past few years to count on one hand. "Declining health" is what the doctors called it. *Has viste Concha? She don't look so good* was another way to put it.

"Conch used to take me and your mom cruisin' in her black Chevy Camaro after school," Lucry told me.

Luc didn't say as to what exactly they did while cruisin' but I imagined it might be the perfect first—and supposedly only—setting for my Mami Maria to get acquainted with Mary Jane, Concha's favorite friend. I didn't press Lucry to spill the details. But I did ask her to paint me a picture of this lowrider. She gladly took to story-mode, full throttle.

"The outside of Concha's ranfla gleamed like gasoline itself. It had plush velvet seats—maroon, maybe. A top-shelf 8-track player for a steady rotation of souldie rolas. Permanent clouds of pot smoke. And. . ." Tia Luc let the silence linger like a too-long-drum roll before the final reveal, "a chain link steering wheel with chrome so clean you could see your whole face in the middle of it."

I imagined dreamy doo-wop tracks in their true analog form, crooning into my tia's ears and spilling out into the streets. Horn-rich California soulsters like the San Francisco TKO's, or anything by Motown queen Mary Wells for the more upbeat drives. I also imagined Zapp and Roger's "Doo Wa Ditty" for cruises with the homegirls.

The last time I had seen Concha was two years prior. She had come through the back-lot entrance of the bomb, hole-in-the-wall Mexican restaurant on Middlefield Road my mom and I were at. I'd just flown in from Portland and my first stop, straight from the SFO airport, was naturally a spot in Redwood City's own Little Mexico for a steaming bowl of morisqueta and my own personal vat of Pacifico michelada. I was mid karaoke croon—*Pero ay yi yi! Como me duele*—when we saw her.

Concha walked in and sat at her own table. "Walked" is a generous description of what her body was capable of doing, her legs having lost full functionality since getting sicker and sicker and requiring a tortoise pace but walked is what she tried. My mom howled wassup over my off-key pocha rendition of Selena, and as soon as I sang my last line, I turned around to give her a kiss on the cheek. Concha said hi back and the kiss was awkward, but it was always awkward to show affection to my tia. On the spectrum of hugs and smooches in our family, Concha held down a cool corner, reserving the love she doled through food, never words. This is typical of us—loud mouthed, but with the emotional vulnerability left at the surface.

We exchanged a few polite words and left shortly after.

In the car with my mom, I asked if she'd talked to Concha recently—if things were still weird between them. She wasn't really sure the answer to either but said nothing ever felt the same between them after that Christmas Eve, half a decade earlier, when my mom had asked Concha if her son had taken my disappeared Christmas money.

I got quiet. My heartbeat quickened, the erupting fizz of a shaken soda. I dissolved into thought. "Asked" is how my mom put it. "Accused" is probably how my tia would've put it.

We had probably seemed like stuck up bougie coconut bitches, making a stink about missing money at the expense of losing trust. Maybe my mom, a seemingly assimilated immigrant living in the burbs, came off like she forgot she grew up in the hood. Maybe my Tia Concha, proud as hell to have grown up and stayed in Redwood City, felt singled out.

I felt the guilt seep in knowing my mom was probably just trying to stick up for me and Tia Concha the same for her own. I wondered if my Mami questioned other parents and where the money ever ended up. Maybe I had misplaced it. Maybe I was responsible for the disbanding of kindred homegirls.

Later that day, we told my sister we ran into Concha and she told us we all ought to reach out more; be there for our tia like she'd been there for us growing up. She said Tia Concha was probably feeling alone through these last few years of declining health and could probably use our support.

I stayed quiet. My mom said they had just drifted apart. It wasn't personal.

We didn't bring up that Christmas. We carried on the Bravo family tradition of cartwheeling away from the truth. Excuses were easier than confrontation or rejection or drudging up a past we'd rather have forgotten.

* * *

When Lucry and I finally made it into the ICU on Christmas Eve 2018, we let Concha's voice guide the way. She wasn't too far from the barrier we'd finally crossed over to get inside, but we found Concha sitting up in bed, propped by pillows, talking loudly. The nurse kept telling her she was going to get better. Concha said she was uncomfortable and needed more nurses to help move her. She didn't seem to notice us.

"You have visitors," the nurse said.

"Ayyye, what up Conch?" Lucry shouted to fill the too-long silence. She walked over to a seat at the side of Concha's bed. I sat by the foot.

It felt ridiculous to ask how Concha was doing, on account of it being Christmas and her being in the hospital again, but it's all I could think of saying. I wanted to talk about anything other than her being sick. I didn't bring up her pre-teen son Jose—how, at first, she and husband didn't want Jose to visit her in the hospital—to see her like this—and how he didn't want to visit now, probably too afraid or sad, though he was more adept at expressing anger.

Lucry is better at moving past small talk and eventually got her talking, letting Concha's own storytelling chops shine. Concha launched into the retelling of her visit to Mexico just a few months prior with my abuelita and tio—her siblings.

She told us all about her first visit to the Motherland: how there was terrible fucking traffic through the mountainous village they were in, how it was hot as hell, how the curbs were busted, and they struggled to push her up over the bumps and cracks in her wheelchair.

They went to see a "fucking witch doctor," as my tia put it. She was never afraid to tell it like it is. Abuelita had probably heard a scammy ass radio ad on La Raza, between Bad Bunny and the bachata, but she convinced her siblings to board a plane to a pueblo in the middle of Michoacán. After a very long journey and wait, they made it to the doctor.

"We finally got into the room where he was doing his operations," Concha said. "The room—it just looked like a room in a tiny goddamn house. It was dark and there were a bunch of fuckin' jars. Then he was speaking Spanish, talking about stem cells, and he holds up a jar with—a fucking baby pig!"

We were doubled over laughing. She was spitting comedy gold and even had the nurses laughing. Concha swore it was all bullshit—the promise of curing all ailments with the implantation of piglet stem cells into the arms of the ill. But she went ahead and tried it anyway with my tio, her own brother, who also has had many brushes with cardiac arrest and open-heart surgeries.

Did she feel any better after? Hell no. But the food? It was real good.

* * *

Between that Christmas and the Super Bowl, Concha didn't get better. I'd get occasional phone calls from my mom updating me on what was happening. My mom showed her love by staying up to date on Concha's health, having long phone calls with the family members taking care of Concha or her family, and visiting Concha herself. She said sometimes she and her siblings would sing oldies, swaying to the beat, at Concha's bedside.

It was a slow, seemingly inevitable but allegedly preventable wind towards another too soon death for our family. She had a case of diabetes—like her brother and sister and nephew— and a series of subsequent complications; cardiac arrest, chronic chronic use, an undying love for the food of our blood—salty, saucy, spicy, cotija cheesy comida Michoacána—and clotted blood that caused her legs to swell and veins to swim with pain.

She underwent a surgery soon after I had seen her to try to intervene in the persistent poor circulation that threatened to leave her with no legs. While recovering from that, the nurses accidentally dropped her while moving her to a new bed, breaking her arm. While recovering from that, the doctors discovered she'd gotten sick with a staph infection. People with diabetes are thought to be at higher risk for staph infections and so are people who spend time in hospitals—the very places folks are supposed to heal, and yet this bacteria likes to live there, preying on weakened immune systems.

After so many years of cycling through suffering and recovery and back, it was the spread of this bacterial infection into her bloodstream that ultimately proved too much for her body to bear.

Right before her life came to an end, I had gotten news at work, via group text, that the doctor's options for intervention had been exhausted. My mom asked us for prayers and punctuated the request with a solemn sad-face emoji.

I excused myself for a break from the non-profit where I was working. I forgot my coat. The cold numbed my face and my arms as I cried and walked as far away from the crowded food carts and tourists as I could to less populated blocks in downtown Portland.

Two hours after the first text, my uncle texted that she was on morphine in room 2112, eyes closed, and not talking besides crying out for help. One hour after that text, I gave a presentation on classroom technology tips for teaching artists. I did a *good* job of compartmentalizing.

Twenty-two hours after my uncle's message, we got another group text from my mom: *Concha just took her last breath May she Rest In Peace.*

I read the thread again a few hours later. I saw silence. I saw whole heart and broken heart emojis in place of words. I saw the small grayed out type: *Lucry left the conversation*. I didn't have words yet either, so I cried again.

* * *

Delfina Bravo Godinez was 57 years old when she passed. Five years and eight years sooner than her own mami and papi had been when they left this world. One teenaged son and a high school sweetheart-turned-husband left behind.

And contrary to what the world wants you—wants us—to think about perpetually sick people coming to terms with their own deaths before crossing over to the other side, Concha did not want to wave her white flag.

Sure, a quicker ending might have looked like an appealing solution after she'd spent months past the promised week in a hospital, feeling her form deteriorate when she was supposed to be healing. She'd spent weeks in antiseptic white rooms surrounded more often by strangers than by family. Strangers who moved from speaking about the future to only asking about pain levels. Nurses that stopped by to ask if she was comfortable, cutting the previous *you'll beat this* pep talks from their scripts. Facing family members who popped by out of the woodwork, iPhones blaring The Supremes and Brenton Wood.

But if it had still been up to Conch, she would have chosen more years living with that agonizing pain, blood poisoned, so she could be there for her family. For her son. So we wouldn't have to play "Tell Him" by Patti Drew in her place.

In the days leading up to the funeral, I found myself feeling like a ghost hovering outside my body. I watched as my fingers pressed the buttons on the massive CD burning tower I'd borrowed, to expedite the memorial mix CD making. I had selected and arranged songs sent in a flurry of texts in a group thread with a Tia Sylvia, Tia Silvia, Tia Lucry, Cousin Adam, Uncle Baby, and my Mom. Tia Silvia also chimed in with thoughts from Jaime, Concha's widower. I located shortened radio versions, mediated track negotiations, and made custom edits to cram as many songs as we could into the 80 allotted minutes.

I told people my aunt died. I didn't feel much of anything. When my boyfriend offered space to talk or his shoulder to cry on, I just hung my head low like I was trying to trick myself, convince myself into sadness. I told my therapist I was a lousy human, focused only on output: one perfectly curated playlist with 80 percent oldies and 20 percent español, 220 iridescent CD faces varnished with matte stickers that matched the Facebook event page and flyer I'd designed—soft pinks, butter yellow flowers, elegant maroon script, and a dewy youthful Delfina with Farrah Fawcett curls. The duties had also fallen on me, as the deemed writer in the family, to edit the eulogy our cousin Lorena wrote and to add comments asking for details when I couldn't summon them myself. Someone asked me to write an obituary. I promised I would soon.

My therapist assured me creating order and making decisions are one way to feel control when it feels like there isn't any. My grief process was to make promises and funeral recuerdos for others to keep remembering Concha.

The day of the funeral, the sky was black and wet. Clouds gleefully dumped buckets of rain onto the heads of the funeral-goers. This, in a town with a hefty promise of a slogan: Climate Best by Government Test!

I wore a black dress, tights, and boots with a golden buckle. I lugged the weight of dozens of jewel cases in paper grocery bags, newly transferred from an extra carry-on suitcase. I placed the CDs in two baskets at the entrance of the church. Then I entered the brown-carpeted chapel and scanned the pews, doing the math as quickly as I could; one niece two generations down with two-hundred mix CDs did not equal row one. I sat in the second. Jaime, Concha's widower, also sat in row two next to me and my grandmother. Little Jose sat in the furthest back row of the church. I thought everyone's math, including mine, was off.

A few minutes into the priest's opening remarks, Jaime turned to me and asked if I could read something on his behalf, simultaneously placing a neatly folded piece of white paper in my hand. It was a goodbye letter scrawled in chicken scratch. A beautiful, raw first-person lover's ode written hurriedly and heavily punctuated with many Babes.

I, like most of my family, have never known Jaime very well. He'd always preferred staying home with his records or spending time with his family over spending time with ours—not out of dislike, but out of a deep like for his own comfort. He preferred to do without small talk and without the mingling. Concha and Jose were his world. Everything else adjacent.

So, at the funeral, I agreed to read on behalf of Jaime. I am not in the business of saying no when grieving people ask for help. I gently unfolded and smoothed out the creases in his origami missive before I headed to the podium. I delivered his ode as best as I could. My muted emotions helped out too.

Later in the service, the priest invited others to speak at the mic. Hundreds were packed into the rows—siblings-in-law, coworkers, school mates and homegirls—familia on all sides. I couldn't find words or stories of my own to share. So, I stayed quiet, listened, and waited. Soon, the mix CD would blare in the reception hall and we'd eat, laugh, sip Modelos, and just groove to the tracks.

* * *

After the funeral, life stayed busy. Time stretched and continued moving. I had the privilege of living. And I also had more time to let my guilt thrive.

The more I thought about the obituary, the bigger it became. Who was I to write this woman's story? How could I write about Delfina Concha Bravo Godinez when I didn't feel I knew enough of the family history, of her history, to possibly summarize her life? Wasn't it a sign that I shouldn't be attempting this when I had to call my Mami every hour I wrote to ask for her take on the facts?

Who was I to let the ink dry on Concha's legacy?

I looked to the Internet to reveal the deeper meanings of death, memorialization, the history of obituaries and who writes them and when and for whom, and *about* whom. I typed, deleted, and repeated questions, hoping to find answers. I researched the origins of the obituary in search of a formula to help me write one of my own. I craved rabbit holes and Wikipedia holes to tumble down and get lost in. I wanted the distraction of infinite knowledge to keep me from my attempts to write. I thought about who has, and has had, the right to have their life memorialized in newspapers. To be remembered in this serious way.

I thought about the Concha I knew and the rose-colored worlds obits in newspapers painted. I thought about Concha and how hard it would be to capture her essence on the page. To capture her wit with so few words. How funny it is to use a word like essence to describe Concha.

I googled the word 'legacy.' I wondered if a legacy that is incorrect is better than none at all. I wondered what it would be worth to write a legacy that's been sanitized, dissolved, censored. Who even would that obituary be *for*?

I almost convinced myself too much time had passed. I tried to find rules that confirmed it was too late. I did not find these rules written although they surely exist unspoken. I had no choice but to try and make good on my promise.

Concha would want me to be real. She'd want to be remembered the way she truly was.

* * *

Delfina "Concha" Bravo attended Sequoia High School where she fell madly in love with her high school sweetheart-turned-husband, Jaime Mora, when she was fifteen years old. She graduated the same year Smokey Robinson's "Cruisin'" made the Billboard Top 100. Her homegirls, self-dubbed the Mary Jane Gang, rocked feathered hair flips and belted Dickie's in a nod to the stylings of their Pachuca foresisters. Concha was a ride or die hyna, and she eternalized her love for her homegirls with a home-poked M.G. tattoo situated precisely in the soft fat of her curled fist, between the left index finger and thumb.

My Tia Concha was unabashedly her fucking self. She lived life on her own terms. If there were slogans for funerals, hers could only be "Laugh Now, Cry Later."

Concha is best remembered as a sarcastic baggy-Raiders-windbreaker-wearing tia in a family full of Niners fans. She had a soft spot for all shades of nostalgia. The cramped studio apartment she lived in with Jaime, above my abuelita's garage, was solely decorated with mountains of record crates (pre-hipster revival), wafts of smoke, and endless stacks of leather-bound photo albums. Conch was always reminiscing on days with her homegirls. The careful archivist, every picture she'd ever taken, it seemed, had a home in her apartment.

Before she was dying, my Tia Concha was the wild, crazy, cool tia to two generations, beginning with my Mami and Tia Lucry, and later to me and my cousins.

Mexican families sprawl so long that your babies have babies before their other siblings are grown, and so you end up with tios and primas and tias and cuñados who are all around the same age. More like a scribbly buncha squiggles of blood than any straight line.

Dare to ask who is related to who and how and you will be met with the slow blinks and eye rolls of deep brown eyes. We are all familia, is the point. No seas tonta.

But if you really want to know, Tia Concha was my abuelita's sister and Tia Lucry is my mom's first cousin, which makes Lucry and Concha both my tias, period.

At family parties, Tia Concha occupied her own table, her own couch, her own world. Growing up, I witnessed her voice, a pendulum, swinging from quiet as hell to loud as hell with a swiftness. It wasn't so much that she ever yelled, but rather her words were weapons she knew how to use just right. Her quietness was purely observational. She was at the ready, equipped to leave you bleeding from her words, shanked in the gut in the blink of an eye, but definitely doubled over laughing too.

When we were little, Concha's favorite contribution to the family was making all the kids' birthday cakes. Pillowy swirls of buttercream frosting and whipped cream with delicately placed strawberries was her specialty. She'd perfectly pipe our names in glorious candy apple red script. They were a highlight reserved for our youth—the newest generation of niños was never bestowed with this gift. The family seems to have since sold out, buying our cakes from hyped up overpriced bakeries off Yelp. Beautiful and delicious no doubt, but never as tasty as one made with love by a tia.

Concha was also always happy to take full advantage of her Peninsula Community Center family pass. She took me and my sister and our cousins Amanda and Monica to this semi-public pool frequently and taught us how white people think brown people all look the same—how if you just wait outside around the corner for five minutes, they'll forget they've already scanned you in, or how if you don't want to wait, you can just open the side gate at the back for all your other primos and tias.

"Okay, Tupaca," she'd say to me when my Tupac-obsessed teenage suburban ass thought I was hood. "Okay, Tupaca," she'd say to me when my *Portlandia* collegiate ass thought I was twee.

She was the epitome of #NoFilter, commenting things like "WTF" and "LMAO" on any posts or photos she found weird. College me was simultaneously mortified by the read and exhilarated by her boldness. She used Facebook as a way to keep in touch with distant cousins and old classmates and was in groups like "You Know You're from Redwood City When" and "Yo amo comida Michoacána." She posted firme, chingona oldies on my timeline—nostalgic bootleg jams uploaded to YouTube with black-and-white Chicano artwork.

She introduced me, back in my own wannabe chola days, to one my all-time favorite songs: "Angel Baby" by Rosie and the Originals. I used to play it on repeat after my frequent heartbreaks and sob through the night into my pillow.

Tia Concha treated us like the kids she never had; she was told her whole life she would never conceive. Then fifteen years ago, after spending months sick and unknowingly pregnant, she was told—surprise!—she could conceive. She eventually pushed out a baby boy we joked she should call Milagro.

Her son is a firecracker like his mama. He is smart and a smart ass. This combination can be lethal, academically speaking. He also finds community on the Internet, connection through music, as a little kid scouring YouTube for Michael Jackson tracks to groove to and now, as a teen, learning how to make his own beats.

We all hoped in those months leading up to her last breath she might have a second chance at miracles. But even near the end, in her own darkest moment, Concha reminded us that life was a gas. And we all could cry it out with an oldie.

* * *

Concha's appearances at Christmas were rare, but she'd pop in on occasion. The emptiness of a Bay Area Christmas without Concha, of knowing she couldn't be there in the flesh if she wanted, was palpable the first year of her being gone and we all missed her. Her son spent the evening slinked back into our aunt's living room couch, stone-faced, low-profile, flying solo as usual. He'd just started high school and was learning Ableton software in a class, the music still in his blood. I tried to be the cool tia, relating, telling him I'm a DJ. "I call myself Mami Miami," I tried to joke. "Oh," was all he said back.

But in true Bravo family style, we didn't talk much more about our feelings. We turned to what works best: blasting heart-wrenching oldies, dripping with nostalgia, to croon out words we can't find the courage to sincerely say on our own.

"Concha loved this song," my tia said as Wendy Rene played.

"Let's pour one out," my cousin Martin whooped!

Lucry cranked up the music. We huddled our solo cups close as a grizzly-haired white uncle sheriff rationed out a handle of Kirkland tequila. All twenty or so of us raised our red plastic chalices and tossed a shot back in her honor. I licked the salt off my hand and let the squeeze of lime slide down my throat. Someone changed the track to Mac Dre. I bent my knees and waved my arms wildly in a subpar attempt to do The Bird.

Jose was still in his own world on the couch.

Concha is still with us all.

* * *

Life is too short to have sorrow
You may be here today and gone tomorrow
You might as well get what you want
So go on and live, baby, go on and live
Tell it like it is
　　　　　　—Aaron Neville, "Tell It Like It Is"

Concha's Mix:
Angel Baby – Rosie & The Originals
Me & You – Brenton Wood
I'm Your Puppet – James & Bobby Purify
You Beat Me To The Punch – Mary Wells
Baby, I'm For Real – The Originals
Let's Stay Together – Al Green
Mary Jane – Rick James
All Night Long – Mary Jane Girls
Whatcha See Is Whatcha Get – The Dramatics
The One Who Really Loves You – Mary Wells
Tell It Like It Is – Aaron Neville
Together – Tierra
La-La Means I Love You – The Delfonics
Sitting in the Park – Billy Stewart
Ooo Baby Baby – Smokey Robinson
Me and Mrs. Jones – Billy Paul
Two Lovers – Mary Wells
Low Rider – War
Oye Como Va – Santana
Suavecito – Malo
Es Demasiado Tarde – Ana Gabriel
Como Quien Pierde Una Estrella – Alejandro Fernández
Volver Volver – Vicente Fernández

15. sea of love

2011

Dear Emilly,

I am so sad to know that you and Dale are no longer a couple. I care for you deeply and want you to know you are always very welcome in my home. I am remembering how I once felt many years ago and how very hurt and unhappy. I was super lucky with Jeff. I saw a therapist a short time before filing for divorce from Bill. He said why had I waited so long. I said "I guess I'm afraid of being lonely." He said, bless him, "you won't be lonely long." And he was right - I wasn't.

And I predict you won't be either.

Much love,
Cyrena

* * *

2014

Hi Cyrena! I hope you are doing well and are happy. This is Emilly Prado, Dale's old girlfriend.

I stumbled across a card you had mailed me following Dale's and my breakup three years ago. Come to think of it, it must be almost 3 years ago on the dot. In it, you wrote that I wouldn't be lonely for long. I never gave you a proper thank you for these kind words, so I wanted to do so now because 3 years late is better than never.

I've since seen the beginning and end of another relationship, but I've found that your statement rings even more true now. Unpartnered, I've found companionship in myself and in friends and family. I'm not lonely as you predicted, but in a way that has surprised me. Thank you for your support and love throughout the years. I hope to see you on one of my next visits to the Bay Area.

I hope year 92 is as wonderful a year as ever.

Sending love from Portland,
Emilly

16. la llorona

IN THE MIDDLE of Mama Coyo's house in Aguililla, Michoacán, there is a tree with thick beige roots buried deep into the ground. Papa Nano lives there too but I have become accustomed to referring to it as her house on account of my own single mother, the single mothers of all my friends, and the true matriarchs running households on both sides of my family.

The tree in the middle of the house is majestic and several feet taller than the roof. Its branches sprout high up through a wide, squared opening in the roof, curling over the kitchen and above the cemented pila holding this week's clean water. The tile that surrounds the tree—the walkway between the kitchen and bathroom—has tilted uphill under its roots. It grew right before our eyes even though no one noticed. If you're not careful and walk too heavy, you can kick a square tile loose.

As kids, we'd climb up the arms of the tree. We'd run to the tree for safety—for protection from Mama Coyo's viciously nippy macaw. One time my sister Daniela wasn't careful enough and tumbled down, so many feet, onto her back. She cried but she did not die. Growing up, I was sure it was because God had been watching.

The hole in the roof of Mama Coyo's house is not an accident. It's more like a broad sunroof made without glass. If I chopped down the tree at the heart of this house, I could count the rings to tell you how old it is, but I can tell you instead that it was more than two embraces wide when I was seven years old. It took almost twenty years before I saw anything else like it—another tree smack in the middle of a house.

In the daytime, el sol beams down, and Papa Nano lays across the plastic-weaved folding chair in the salon, warmed and swatting flies in his sleep. I have never seen Papa Nano's eyes because he hides them behind thick black sunglasses, having lost one to a dart or maybe a stick as a kid, but I am sure he is asleep when I see him lying there (at least some of the time).

At night, the stars glimmer and the black shadows of fleeting birds and bats dash overhead. The tree at the heart of the house continues to grow and happily laps up the rainwater when it pours. Unlike me, the tree is not afraid; Not of the water or the lightning or the thunder that shuts off our electricity and shakes the other two-toned houses around. When I was still little in every way, my tiny body would shake as I cried and covered my ears, holding my breath when the flashes brought light and the dread of a mounting roar.

I was taught to be less scared because Mama Coyo told me in Spanish that God built an invisible barrier around this pueblo to protect it from being burned by lightning strikes. She'd tell me how this pueblo had existed for thousands of years and not once did it get burned to a crisp or crack under a bolt of ice-white relámpago.

* * *

This house is where my Papi grew up when he was blonde and blue-eyed for the first two years of his life. This is where my Papi continued to grow when his hair turned black and his skin turned brown and he lost two of his nine siblings: one from a gunshot and another from a scorpion sting insider her baby cuna. This is the house I spent my summers in, growing up and into my morena skin and learning the feeling of what it's like to blend in for the first time.

In Mexico, I learned the nicknames of every kid on the block and wore my own name proudly. My Papi must have called me his Flaca the first time he laid eyes on me—a slippery and noodley 22 inches long, 6 lbs. light. "Skinny Girl" doesn't have the same ring to it, like so many other words that lose their poesy by way of translation, but his Skinny Girl I was.

In Aguililla, I was also Flaca, and there was the loud and wildly goofy Chucho. The rude ass, gold-chain wearing bully was called Carlingas. Across the way were Ticho y Toco, the older neighborhood sisters-turned-lifetime family friends (one of which I witnessed pretending to be my aunt when my family helped her cross the border as I sat in the back row of our Suburban), and a few blocks further out lived Canelo, the cinnamon-haired, amply freckled moreno. Plus, my little brothers, Flaco (Hector) and Gordo (Hector) were also named on account of their weight.

My Papi was given the nickname of Chayote when he emerged from the womb with hair eternally reaching high up into the sky. His strands the prickly spikes of the chayote vegetable—known in English less beautifully as the mirliton squash. My mom's nickname is Chatiya—a nickname passed down from her own mother's nickname of Chata, and one given to people blessed with allegedly funny noses. My Tia Delfina was always known as Concha and when she died, my family wrote it on her funeral invitation with pride.

Having witnessed nicknames lasting lifetimes, and up to and beyond the grave, I did not know names could have an expiration date until my own had come and gone. I do not know when my own *Flaca* was annulled, but maybe it was right after my 21st birthday? There was no coroner or grim reaper who appeared after the scale passed a certain number nor a memo sent from my father alerting me my nickname was dead.

What is the name for a grief that creeps in after losing something, mixed with the back-dated guilt and shame of not really noticing? What is the nickname for a person who no longer embodies their name? What happens to a person who has become unrecognizable to some? What do we call a tree that's been severed from its roots? A person who has been robbed of their identity?

* * *

Men in my family have come up to me to tell me I am no longer Flaca. Women in my family have told me this too. When I told my mom a mustached man—some distant relative—approached me at my Papa Nano's birthday party and said he remembered "when I *used* to be spaghetti," my Mami laughed.

"Spaghetti!" she cackled.

"Spaghetti!" she repeated the punchline back several times. But when my mom stops laughing, she tells anyone who will listen that she used to be spaghetti too. I am mad at the mustached man, but I am even more mad at the mustached man for the sake of my Mami.

Maybe I should have realized my provisional nickname was a challenge. The two syllables a double-edged sword yielding adoration and taunting—daring me to live up to my name. To govern the food that touches my lips when I can no longer eat "without consequence."

Fla-kah. A hissing reminder that I should hunch to make myself seem smaller and that giving up on counting calories meant giving up on who I was born to be.

Flaca is a name to be earned and not a name for the weak. Flaca is not even given to girls or women who are "average," or who teeter to the other side of BMI. Flaca is not to be given to girls who look like me.

* * *

Sometimes I wonder what being seen as skinny again would give me. What I'd get in return—if only I was thinner, if only my kind of *overweight* didn't result in a belly as rolly, if only my hips didn't jut out disrupting that Kim K hourglass illusion—the only figure thicker girls are allowed to have. Sometimes I wonder what ribbons I'd win, what clothes *Cosmo* magazine would tell me I could finally wear, what it would take for Papi to rechristen me as Flaca again. And then I remember there has never been a time I believed I lived up to my nickname of Flaca. There was never a time I looked down at myself and thought, "This body is so beautiful. I am *such* a skinny girl."

There was never a time I was at peace with my body when I was convinced all I needed was to be at war. There was only the time when accidentally starving myself became purposely starving myself. The years when my Mami called me *an anorexic* without knowing how to take it more seriously, or help. The sophomore year of high school dotted by walking pneumonia, a sinus infection, and half a dozen colds in the span of six months. The many seasons of feeling perpetually cold. The day nearing high school graduation when I looked up the signs of suffering from an eating disorder and checked off my matching symptoms (thinning hair, brittle nails, easily bruised, low immune system, low self-esteem). The same day as my matching symptoms when I told myself going through formal treatment wasn't an option because of cost and sure-to-mortify family chisme. There was also the near-decade of falsely thinking all recovery meant was forcing food into my body. In the years since, when grocery store shopping still felt like an impossible math equation—every bagged item another calculation. Even now, when I feel like I'm constantly scanning my thoughts for corruption, filter what media and celebrity accounts I consume, and even though my fear of relapse still follows, I continue to search for my own version of healing.

* * *

This house in Aguililla has witnessed and cycled right alongside my own family's births, growth, and deaths.

I have not been back to this house in at least twelve years, but I have heard it, like me, looks different. My cousins tell me Mama Coyo has a new macaw, still as vicious as the last. Mama Coyo has retired from making cheese. The cows Papa Nano once herded back into the small rancho next to the house have been replaced by parked cars. And they've maybe closed up the opening in the roof, chopping down the once-sprawling tree. I think this is what change looks like. All I can think of is what's gone.

This house is a casket where I will lay Flaca and las vacas and Maya Coyo's first macaw to rest. At the funeral, I will dig a hole into the foundation and drop each letter of my old name, one-by-one. I will stir the dirt with the remains of tree roots and say a prayer for us all—for old time's sakes. At the funeral, there will be no procession or eulogy. No explanations necessary. And for once, I won't be wearing all black.

17. quiero bailar

REGUETÓN SHAKES MY friend Michelle's boyfriend's rock and gem collection in the bedroom of their Bed-Stuy apartment. With every tra and every pa, the music says, "I am here. Aquí andamos." The bass thumps, making the leaves of their happy green house plants, fed and quenched, begin to tremble. The hand claps make their kitchen cupboard shake.

"It is loud," Michelle says. The tra y el pa of her upstairs neighbor happens every day and every night, she says.

I read *Making Rent In Bed-Stuy* by Brandon Harris *loudly* without making a sound: I hold the book, cover splayed, up to my eyes; on the subway, at the art opening, and on Michelle's living room floor, for everyone to see.

"Did you know Bed-Stuy was once ruled by Blacks and Dominicans and Puerto Ricans," I say to her wide-eyed friends during a lull between bands at an art show in another part of Brooklyn. They nod their heads solemnly. They can't *believe* developers keep swallowing up the land. They can't *believe* landlords are to overlords as tenants are to peasants. *They can't believe it has gotten so bad.*

I do not tell them this Bed-Stuy memoir wasn't written by someone born on these blocks. I do not tell them Bedford-Stuyvesant has always fought my mouth, never slipping loosely from my teeth or rolling off my tongue with ease.

* * *

One out of eight of my friends who lives in Bed-Stuy is not white. Seven out of eight of my friends who live in Bed-Stuy are white. Five out of eight friends here say they are artists. Michelle is both white and an artist. Is this neighborhood supposed to be their blank canvas?

New York City is not supposed to look like the world depicted in *Girls*. I have only been here as many times as the fingers on my right hand, but I know New York City is not supposed to look like *Girls*. I think I have landed in *Girls*, but if Hannah liked dancing on her own to Siouxsie instead of Robyn.

Maybe if Michelle's neighbors play their music loudly and if they continue to exist loudly, they will never be forgotten, not be pushed aside.

I am not from Bed-Stuy, but I know where this music comes from.

18. it's my brown skin

I WANT TO know what parts of me are evil. I want to know which parts of my body I should push away and which parts of my body I should hold close. Quiero saber qué partes de mi cuerpo fueron nacido de la tierra. From la mama pacha. From the green lakes and golden marigolds of Michoacán. Not from the rolling hills of Spain.

The pixelized map of the earth informs me I am roughly one-part indigena, two-parts colonizadora. A blend of resilience and violence. Stories of uprising and rebellion, slaughter and suppression buried deep within my veins. A comprehensive history of the conflicting Americas coursing through my own blood.

Ancestry.com reports I am more of my father than I am of my mother. It also tells me I am definitely more white than anything else; My cells are precisely 60 percent European, 33 percent Native, and 7 percent African.

When I mailed off my plastic tube of spit, I hoped my DNA would yield somewhat uncomplicated results. Perhaps the name of a tribe or the names of dead loved ones. An insight into my father's blonde-turned-black hair, or another long-lost half-sibling; further evidence of my Papi's womanizing past. Maybe the discovery of a new tiny town from which I might further trace our roots.

Instead, I discover one-third of my body can be traced to an unwieldy, semi-opaque turquoise blob spanning the stretches of the Americas. The rest of me is a microscopic patchwork of los españoles, europeos, y africanos.

I wonder what my future will look like now that I have discovered, despite the cafecito of my piel and the way I've been treated, I am, indeed, white. I wonder if this is God's sick way of finally answering my prayers—if He gets off on playing games with my sense of self. I wonder who will believe me.

* * *

Scripted commercials and real-life conversations about Ancestry. com revolve around the uncomplicated DNA of white people. *It turns out I'm part Swedish—no wonder I'm so in love with*

minimalist design! My great-grandmother was half-Italian—makes
sense why I'm obsessed with drinking really good coffee.

They, and I, are supposed to be given answers.

But my Ancestry.com results are not so innocuous. My DNA story does not reveal why I love black coffee or particleboard IKEA furniture. My DNA story screams, "You are created from centuries of colonization; the backs of Black and brown people are your stepping-stone."

I do not receive answers. I only receive more questions.

I want to know if my fingernails are Tarascan or Purépecha. I want to know if my teeth were formed from the sandy shores of Northern Spain—if the flesh of my gums are descendants of the Aztecs. If the lines on my elbow were shaped from my Senegalese.

I want to know what language my abuela's abuela—my tatarabuela—spoke before her tongue was cut out. Which ancestors represent the dirt that gathers behind my ears. Which ancestors represent the blood that pours from my left nostril.

I want to know why the colonization of the Americas is a Catch-22: settler borders and blood quantum separating Native Americans from other original peoples stretching wide, across our land mass. Why colonization stays steady conspiring; chugging along to keep our ancestral roots buried.

I want to know if the darkness I call "the Prado anger" is a transfer, passed down from the crimes of our ancestors. I want to know what it would sound like to say my name if my blood, and our hands, were fully clean. I want to know if we come from a people who are cursed.

I want to know which ones of my ancestors' descendants are good, but I am too afraid to know who might be bad. I want to know who my ancestors were. I am also too afraid to ask.

I want to tell my ancestors, "Mira, aquí todavía estamos." I want to tell my ancestors I still dream in Spanish. I want to tell my ancestors I am so angry they raped and tried to eradicate, decimate my other ancestors. I want to tell my ancestors they are so fucking confusing.

I want to scream at Ancestry.com because he did not give me my ancestors' good stories. I want to know who the fuck Ancestry.com thinks he is, rewriting what I have come to know about myself—erasing everything I have been taught.

But I want to know how I can find peace. Even when I hate parts of myself for killing off other parts of myself. Even when I don't know whose side I can take as my own. Even when I want to know which ways to slice and carve the evil from my bones—from my body. Even when I still want to know which parts of my body are truly mine.

19. mad

My therapist asks me how I feel about healing. I pause for too long. I stretch a "hmmmm well" as my mind teeters between calculations, turning over answers so quickly they melt into each other and become putty.

I string together something about defeat, that it feels like it's out of reach, and that I reject the idea that states of being or harm can be fixed. I think healing sounds nice, but it sounds aspirational. I'm not sure what healed looks like. I forget to mention my answer changes depending on the day.

She asks if I feel angry. I say I do. To have healing means to have been harmed. Healing invokes hurt. I am mad. I'd prefer to have been preserved whole.

I don't name the people or the systems aloud, but they flood me at once. When I was five. When I was six. When I was seven, eight, nine, ten. Sixteen. When I was born. Today. Tomorrow.

I listen to a podcast about forgiveness. I think this might be a step towards healing, but there might be nothing I hate more than to be asked for forgiveness. The audacity of a request to be absolved. I am no priest. I will not prescribe a few rote Hail

Marys and eternal repentance. Forgiveness is mine and mine only. It will not be granted. It will not be doled. It will not be summoned by anyone other than myself.

Forgiveness is For White People. I conjure crisp essay theses, sentences, and titles. *In Defense of the School Yard Bully.* I log them as fragments in my Notes app. *When Your Heroes Harm.*

I think they are profound. But when I get around to trying to write them more fully, they often feel empty and small. I can't recall the part of my brain that was so sure of a sentence. The part that was sure I would and could return to flesh out the thought.

It's not that I no longer believe forgiveness is for white people. It's that I don't know if I know what forgiveness is.

I know what it is not: an apology or accountability.

"The journey to release all grudges, to relinquish the quest for revenge, and to let go of the fantasy of what might have been, is one of the most difficult spiritual challenges we will ever face," Oprah Winfrey says of forgiveness on her podcast, *Super Soul Conversations.* "The other side of forgiveness is freedom." I think this sounds nice.

When I was in fifth grade, Mrs. Rook assigned a state research project to our class. We could pick any state except California. The coolest ones were claimed first: Hawaii, New York, Texas, Alaska. I kept my noodley fingers crossed and got my pick: Illinois. The state my Papi lived in. My Mami took me to Walgreen's and let me get the thick fancy black foam board and sheets of thin red, white, and blue. I made the poster post-9/11 patriotic. I cut out squares and stars and used our printer instead of my messy handwriting to make sure my message was clear. I used AOL and checked out nonfiction books from our school library. I covered my ground: state flower, motto, flag, nickname, governor. I picked Oprah Winfrey for 'famous person.' I wrote that Oprah grew up in poverty and was raised by a single mom. She was raped as a child. Then she became one of the richest celebrities through her own hard work, her own version of an American dream.

I wrote that me and my mom watched *The Oprah Winfrey Show* together, which (in 2001) had been on television more than one-and-a-half times as long as I'd been alive. Oprah helps people with her show. At that time, she had lived in Chicago for 17 years and will live there for another decade.

I get a 'B' on my project because Oprah was not born in Illinois. I still haven't forgiven Mrs. Rook.

* * *

Outstretched on a woven blanket I bought on a visit back to the motherland, I listen, ten feet apart, to my friend who sits cross-legged on a blanket of her own. We have removed our pandemic masks and sip iced coffee from plastic cups. She wears all black: two French braids and a long sleeve under her overalls. I wear buttery hues—a plush leopard print tank top and gold door knocker earrings. The Portland sun is out. We're surprised by our own sweat. Sunflowers, stretching higher than the distance between my friend and I, protect us from the noise of the street. Every time I look at my friend, I am looking at art.

We're imagining a world without police. Breonna Taylor and George Floyd and Ahmaud Arbery have just been brutally murdered by cops for being Black. Our community hosts a violin vigil for Elijah McClain. We're talking through the logistics of what a justice system might look like if it were truly just. She is so sure it is possible, and I am so sure I want to be convinced. She entertains my many what ifs.

I tell her I recently learned the name for transformative justice, something I've felt in my bones but never knew how to put to words. I had sent an educational YouTube series via Slack to colleagues after I, the sole person of color in the room, had to listen to eight white people talk about equity work in a meeting, as if it were a new à la carte offering. adrienne maree brown is one of the people interviewed in the videos. I tell my friend I am excited she has written a new book: *We Will Not Cancel Us.* I tell my friend I found the videos as a way to communicate accountability.

When I think about transformative justice, I think about the young men who opened their hearts to me at MacLaren Youth Correctional Facility the couple of times I've visited. It was always a Friday night. I'd carpool for ninety minutes with Carlos, the dope Chicano journalist-turned-Executive Director who started Morpheus Youth Project in 2005. It's a program that supports young people who are incarcerated or who live in underserved communities. His programming is about community, care, and hip hop as replacements for gang life. The guys at MacLaren talked with me about the school-to-prison pipeline, racism, abuse, the prison industrial complex on my visits. We talked about their lives. Who they were before. Who they are now.

The young men, mostly Black and brown, offered acceptance of their mistakes without being asked. It is uncouth to ask, and I know that part of their story isn't for me. But they share that they have caused harmed and say if they could go back, they'd want to make different choices. They understand more about the individual choices within but also the systems that urged their mistakes. From the outside, it seems the lessons have been learned. But mandated years and minimum sentences are not for lessons or epiphanies. They are for hardening.

The first time I leave all I can think is *I get to go home.* Carlos and I get to eat tacos on a carpool pitstop. And they are still there.

I splice together a broadcast journalism piece for a community radio station's Juneteenth programming that blends personal testimony with a recounting of our state and country's racist history. Despite the façade of contemporary progressive politics,

Oregon is second place in the rate of incarcerated youth being directly transferred to adult prisons, by design. Later, I write an article about the power and kinship that is b-boying and why Morpheus Youth Project centers it in their approach. I write about Tyler and Trey and Ephraim. Young men who miss the humans who love them and who are locked up, unable to parent their own children, care for mothers dying of cancer, or be filled with the emotionality and physicality of love. Young men arrested in chrysalis from the full metamorphosis they crave.

The editor at the publication reads my first draft, says there are too many "characters," and asks could I consider cutting one out? I do not think I've made my point clear enough.

* * *

In the park, under the sun, my friend and I discuss the logistics of a victim- or survivor-led process. I accept that I can't change what has happened to me or my body, but I share my biggest wish is that this never happens to another person. Another victim forced into the hardness of survival.

If I don't think prison is a place where humans become better people, I know prison is not the place for my rapist. But I tell her I can't imagine what accountability would look like to me.

She gently nudges me to try.

We dream a scenario where his partner, mother, and the mutual friend who invited and introduced him to me at the party learn about the many wounds he has carved into women. They learn that I am the second person he has sexually violated, at least that I know of, but there are likely more. This white man must remove "feminist" and "activist" from his Twitter bio and bid farewell to his 8,063 followers. His progressive platform has been built on lies (although Herman's having written a television ad, and more, for the man who ran for Portland mayor and lost because he punched a woman when she rejected his sexual advances feels fitting now).

The ink dries on a notarized contract he's signed that ensures I'll never be barred from telling my story. He is sentenced to his own therapy and to paying for mine.

I develop a formula:

(Years Since the Assault x Biweekly Therapy Sessions) x The Cost of Therapy

I apply it and round up:

(8 years x 26 sessions) x 90 dollars = $18,720 of restitution

I wonder how to quantify the attempted assault I survived which my therapist assures counts as trauma too. Maybe I could try to count the involuntary flinches from grazed thighs or fingertips on my neck or the times I've driven by and subsequently shuddered at the Broadway Street bar where I agreed to a second drink before it felt truly scary. Perhaps I might come up with a similar formula but reduce it by half since this assault is the mere ghost of almost.

I try to imagine my idea of accountability as reality and, like healing, it still feels just a little bit out of reach.

* * *

Five months after envisioning, I get an email the week of Thanksgiving from a white man representing a collective whose name means non-violence in Sanskrit. A white woman is CC'd.

I am at my second-hand kitchen table in the middle of learning about strategy and how I might use it to actualize a woodland retreat center I'd like to create with my partner for BIPOC artists in the near future. 2020 has been a year of hibernation and dreaming new ways of being. I see a space where food sovereignty can flourish and where farmers tend to the land in exchange for a bit of produce to feed the community who gathers together to find time to rest and create. I am inspired by the many incredible Black and Indigenous farmers in Portland and want to join them in the tending—of widening access to wholesome foods and safe places to rest for our community.

The email says the white man who raped me seeks greater accountability around the harm he knows he has caused me. They use his full name. They say he's written a letter to me. They mention if I don't reply, they won't bother me again. They never use the word rape or assault. They never explain why this white man thinks he is above our existing systems of justice, or why this white man and these white strangers believe that they get to be part of new systems. Finally, they say their process centers the needs of the person who has been harmed.

My heartbeat quickens. I sink back into the familiar world where nothing else exists but the bar and my bedroom and the car ride and the couch and the bus and the firing and at first only Herman but then Curtis and the bars and the lipstick and the same car too. There is just the black on white of this email. I re-read his name. There is no noise. My face is drenched.

Then, the sudden shriek of a tea kettle boiling over. My anxiety skyrockets right alongside its whistle. I want to let out a scream louder than it can muster.

My boyfriend holds me when I need him to. I jerk away when he makes the mistake of trying to hold me in this moment.

I spend three hours on the Internet trying to find answers or comfort. I can't remember which of my friends have been raped or who would understand. I feel utterly alone. I read "A Survivor's Case Against Restorative Justice" by my new friend, Olivia Pace. I post in private Facebook groups asking where I can find the spaces for BIPOC survivors that are closed to cis men. My string of attributes yields no results.

I try to place the source of my rage. He has been talking about me. He thinks he can be absolved by a group of white people in a subpar collective. A letter is the equivalent of talked at—not listened to. How the fuck does he think he can write a letter when he has no idea how I feel? This is social justice theater masquerading as transformative justice. They use the word restorative—don't they know that's not the same? This is not trauma-informed.

I keep spiraling.

I am lying in the dark with just the sound of a humming laptop. My cheeks feel swollen, like I'm fighting a fever.

My love knows to bring me mint tea with raw honey when I fall back into despair like this. He knows there are times in this world where I still can't bear to be touched. When the only company I can handle is my own. He leaves the tea with an "I love you," and nothing more.

I text Olivia. I try to get out of my spiral. I send an email demanding accountability for this shitty email.

When I leave my bedroom, I find I have been shown love again with sustenance—the thing I always forgo when everything feels out of control. Yellow curry, white rice, pad se ew, tom kha, my partner, and our pit bull are waiting.

* * *

On the second session with my therapist, she says I meet the qualifications for a PTSD diagnosis after conducting a screening. The week before, she (a biracial woman) told me women and femmes of color are underdiagnosed. Before the screening she said women tend to minimize their experiences. She posits scenarios and asks me to rank how frequently they occur in my life on a five-point scale. When I teeter between two numbers a few times, I still go with whatever's lower.

Before I can question the methodology and if my experience really counts, she explains the two techniques for calculation and the minimum scores for each. I rank above average both ways.

I am surprised. I thought the way my body reacted was *normal* even though I knew it felt so wrong and visceral in those moments. I must reckon with what this means. My therapist friends say diagnoses can help guide rather than define. They ask how I feel with the diagnosis, if I identify with it. I thought diagnoses pick you—not the other way around?

I tell my mom about the PTSD on a phone call five days later. I was tempted to withhold this news out of fear she'd judge, or worse, question. But my restlessness and need for comfort, and to be mothered, eats at me more.

She asks me the same first question I asked my therapist: *Is this something I'll live with forever?*

I try to explain, but I don't know enough yet. I think it is like my eating disorder, always looming and calling my name, but I do not tell her this. I tell her I think it will always be there, but hopefully not as bad. I tell her a bit of what the handful of incidents—of being triggered—have felt like. How the separate incidents started to feel the same. How I felt the familiar terror-induced overwhelm of my body again when an online stalker showed up at my work. How I felt that same disembodiment again when I was diagnosed with racial trauma. How I thought it would maybe just go away on its own.

My mom says she is so sorry. She surprises me with her compassion.

"Some brains are just wired differently," she says. "It's just random. Some are stronger."

"Different," I whisper. "Not strong or weak."

* * *

My therapist has been gently nudging me to envision healing. I want healing to mean reversal, and I want to believe it means permanent protection. I'm not sure I, or anyone, has ever known healing in this definition, so I think that definition is wrong. I think healing might mean stability. I think resilience and being able to bounce back from the triggers that may always come up will help. I think healing involves picking at scabs and sometimes turning scars back into scabs so they can become smaller. I think healing might mean turning over the truth and rewriting our memories. I hope healing doesn't mean my erasure.

I am realizing my twenties have been about surviving. I am starting to realize my thirties can be about healing.

* * *

Monarcas molt five times before burrowing into their cocoons.

I wish I knew I'd had my last bite of milkweed.

I think forgiveness may be the final shedding.

I think I am still stuck in chrysalis.

I know the strawflowers are waiting.

00. outro

I'D LIKE TO begin by thanking the woman who brought me into this world: gracias Mami for always believing in me, and for believing I was a writer even when I didn't yet. Thank you for telling me I should be a writer, over and over, until I listened. I'm in awe of your resilience and your willingness to be open and vulnerable during the many sporadic phone calls of poking around at our often-painful past, helping me find the answers I was looking for so I could write this book as truthfully, wholly as possible. I am inspired by your continued commitment to listen and remain open to change. Thank you for everything you have done for me and my siblings. Thank you for being an incredible single mama, and for being there for me, in your own way, even when I couldn't yet communicate my gratitude for you in the way you deserve. I love you. *You are appreciated.*

Thank you to my Papi for making so many smart, beautiful children. You've gifted me with a whole crew of supportive siblings. (I love you E, D, H, H, P, and V). I still want to hear so many of your stories. I love you and hope we can get to know each other better again one day. Special thanks to my oldest sis,

Erika, for being so supportive of my writing, reading all my articles, and making a special display of my books and zines in mom's vitrina! Thanks for encouraging me to keep going and for being there to share stories, fact check, *correct*, and make me laugh.

Gracias a mi abuelita Maria por tu valor y sacrificios: Has hecho el camino para que yo, y todo nuestro familia, pueda vivir la vida llena, creativa y libre—una vida que tu no tuviste la misma oportunidad de vivir. Tambien mando gracias, amor, y gratitude a mi Mama Coyo y Papa Nano en Michoacán—les extraño mucho y estoy agradecida por sus sacrificios y fuerza mismo.

Infinite thanks to my partner and favorite dog dad, César, who has fed me countless homemade meals, freshly-brewed cups of coffee, and tended to the home we've created so that I could immerse myself into the writing process. Thank you for acting as a deeply thoughtful, insightful, and kind on-call editor. I love you so much. You bring so much to this world, our home, and I'm grateful to get to do life with you. I owe many belly rubs and puppuccinos to our dog son, Hemy, for also always being there for a much-needed snuggle, walk, or as my body pillow for the many naps writing this book required.

Thank you to Kevin Sampsell—editor, small press and literary enthusiast, publisher of Future Tense Books. You've helped give this collection a new life, offered so many reads peppered with insightful questions and edit suggestions, and have given this book—and the books of so many other emerging writers—the welcome it was yearning for. Thank you to Francisco Morales for your collaboration and for creating such beautiful art for *Funeral for Flaca*. Your work is always fuego, and this cover is no exception! Thank you Emma Alden and Alexandria Gonzales—FFF interns extraordinaire! You've both helped make vital connections, lend your sharp editorial eyes, and ship out so many of these books.

Looking forward to all that's bright and literary in your near futures.

Thank you to my quarantine-formed BIPOC writing group for your tenderness, giving feedback on many of the new essays, and keeping the fire fueled for us all to stay writing: Vanessa Micale, Tara Noronha, Dez Ramirez, Jen Shin, Ari Schill. (Readers—keep your eyes peeled for their work!) I'd also like to thank Alley Pezanoski-Browne and Harper Quinn of the Independent Publishing Resource Center for administering the Prose Certificate Program, the many workshop instructors who patiently taught me how to make the first iteration of the book, the late journalist, Debby Rankin, whose work is worthy of celebrating on its own and whose scholarship directly funded my participation in the program and supported the creation of this book. To my incredible IPRC instructor, Margaret Malone, I can't thank you enough. You poured yourself into supporting another cohort of writers, helped me see writing in a new way, and paved a crucial path for my development as a writer. Thanks to Margaret for also pairing me with Sara Guest as a mentor. Sara, thank you for hitting the ground running with me as I burned the midnight oil in making this book. You've gone above and beyond with your support and I can't thank you enough for stepping up to offer your crucial copy-editing skills—In 2019 and again in 2021. Big ups to my IPRC crew—I'm so appreciative of the care you each put into giving insightful feedback on my work: Karina Agbisit, Raveena Bhalara, Shannon Edwards, Joe Galván, Sara Kachelman, Kasie Shahbaz, Diana Sharp. I can't wait to read more of your work and see your next books and stories out in the world.

Thanks also the writers who I've had the opportunity to learn from in workshops over the years—Denise Chavez, Kali Fajardo-Anstine, Janice Lee, Rios de la Luz, Katherine Standefer, Elissa Washuta, Lidia Yuknavitch—and the countless other writers I have learned from through their lectures and work. So many editors, but special shout out to Kjerstin Johnson who I had the pleasure of interning with at *Bitch Media* and have continued to be in community with. Thank you, Lance Cleland at *Tin House*, for persistently including me in your special community of writers too.

I'd be remiss not to include formal thanks and acknowledgments to some of the activists, writers, and artists who have helped me find a path to healing and shaped my own political lens: bell hooks, Gloria Anzaldúa and especially *This Bridge Called my Back*, the many years of bomb writing in *Bitch Media* and the *Crunk Feminist Collective* blog, Dr. Angela Davis, Sonya Renee Taylor and her book *The Body is Not an Apology*, Gloria Lucas of Nalgona Positivity Pride, Cory Lira, adrienne maree brown, Assata Shakur, Tarana Burke—creator of #MeToo, Michaela Coel's *I May Destroy You*, Kimberelé Williams Crenshaw—creator of the intersectionality framework, Vy Hồng Phạm, my two favorite therapists (2012-14; 2021-present), the poetry of Tupac Shakur, and too many other musicians to list. **Black Lives Matter. La vidas negras importan.**

Last, but not least, thank you, reader, for taking the time to pick up this book. For reading my words. For supporting me as a writer. For believing in my stories too.

EMILLY GISELLE PRADO is a writer, DJ, and educator living in Portland, Oregon. She is a first-and-a-half generation Chicana, raised in the San Francisco Bay Area by a first-generation Mexican American and a Mexican immigrant from Michoacán. As an award-winning multimedia journalist, Emilly spent half a decade reporting on stories typically centered on amplifying the voices and experiences of people from marginalized communities. Her writing has appeared in nearly 30 publications including *NPR, Marie Claire, Bitch Media, Remezcla, Eater, The Oregonian, The Stranger, Oxygen,* and *Travel Oregon*. Emilly is the author of *Examining Assimilation* (Enslow, 2019), a youth non-fiction book at the intersections of identity and U.S. history. She is a Blackburn Fellow and MFA candidate at Randolph College, and a previous Community Stories Fellow awarded in partnership with Oregon Humanities, the Andrew W. Mellon Foundation, and the Pulitzer Prizes. She serves as Director of Youth Programs at Literary Arts, co-founder of Portland in Color, and moonlights as DJ Mami Miami with Noche Libre, the Latinx DJ collective she co-founded in 2017. Find her online @emillygprado and at www.emillyprado.com.

Future Tense Books

Portland, Oregon

FUTURETENSEBOOKS.COM